from the

Father's Heart

Joy & Adventure

DAILY DEVOTIONAL

Tailored for Life's Seasons -
Emotionally & Spiritually

MARIA KEAR

From the Father's Heart (Book 3)
Joy & Adventure - Daily Devotional
Tailored for Life's Seasons —
Emotionally and Spiritually.

First Edition June 2025

STM Press
    978-1-966240-04-4 (paperback)
    978-1-966240-05-1 (ebook)

*All scripture references are from the New
Living Translation unless otherwise noted.*

*All word definitions were taken from the
Strong's Online Concordance unless
otherwise noted.*

Designed by Suzanne Parrott
Cover Image created using Midjourney

**From the
Father's Heart
series**

Rest & Reflection
Growth & Healing
Joy & Adventure
Hope & Possibilities

Acknowledgements

I want to thank my 5 family – Jeff, Matthew, Katherine and Abigail (I'm the 5th) for always cheering me on when I have crazy ideas like writing my own books. Even if they think I'm weird, they still love me.

I want to thank Debra Rothrock and Angie Davidson for their eyes on the text when they had a moment to make sure my grammar and punctuation were in line.

I want to thank Suzanne Fyhrie Parrott for being my publishing partner and the one who made all the details come together so my voice could be heard in the earth.

Dedication

This book is dedicated to the current and future Jesus lovers who will never tire of reading God's Words or of hearing Him speak. To the ones who love and seek out adventure with Holy Spirit as guide and partner. To the ones who are not satisfied with only what this world offers, but long for news from their place of origin – Heaven. And to those brave enough to hug their Bibles to their chests with wide smiles and tear-stained faces. You have found your people!

Author's Note

The first book I learned to read was the King James Version of the Holy Bible. I was five years old when I picked up the book and just started reading. My mom told me that no one taught me to read, but that I just started reading one day.

When I asked her how that was possible, she replied that from the moment I came home from the hospital to live with her and my grandparents Wheeler in Meggett, SC, my granddaddy Wheeler read to me, making sure I could see each page and picture as he read. We believe that his gift of reading to me from day one prepared my brain to be an early and life-long lover of books, especially the Bible.

Thank you, Granddaddy Wheeler.

Day 183

Somebody Told a Lie about Me

2 Kings 20:1-22:2 / Acts 21:18-36 / Psalm 150 / Proverbs 18:9-10

The word "false" is defined in the Oxford Dictionary as "not according with truth, deliberately meant to deceive, treacherous or unfaithful." "Accusation" is defined as "a charge or claim that someone has done something illegal or wrong." A false accusation according to these two definitions almost looks like a double negative since neither is positive in nature. When we accuse someone of something, we are never complimentary.

In Acts 21 Paul was being accused of preaching and telling the Jews not to follow the law, which he was not doing. The text doesn't say why Paul was being accused or even who was accusing him.

It states in verse 21 that "the Jewish believers here in Jerusalem have been told..." By whom? It sounds like hearsay is coming alongside these false accusations.

What was the motive behind the false accusation? We don't have an answer to that either, although many times in scripture it was the religious leaders who were bringing accusations based on jealousy. So, maybe that was the "who" and the "why" in this case.

There was another man in scripture who was falsely accused. The religious leaders accused Him of blasphemy of being God or of being equal with God. That's because they were not able to see that Jesus was God who had come to earth in the form of mankind. The religious leaders in this case were jealous because Jesus had people who believed His teaching and were following Him.

What about you? Have you ever been falsely accused? I always say it's hard enough to be harassed for the things I have done, but my goodness why must I be harassed for things I did not do? When I feel this way, I'm reminded that I'm in good company with Paul and Jesus. I'm sure many other believers throughout the centuries have also been falsely accused.

Maybe there is no answer to the question of "why" we are being accused. Maybe we need to learn to respond with humility and not anger. Maybe we need to, instead of accusing others, ask questions to find out the truth. I'm learning that asking questions allows me to find out that I may have misunderstood the situation.

When my children were small, I taught them to come into a room with their mouths closed, then assess what's happening before they spoke. What if we did that with one another? What if we kept our mouths closed, listened, asked good questions and most importantly asked God for wisdom in hearing what is really happening in a situation.

You know that old saying we have in our court system, "innocent until proven guilty." We must treat others that way! We must not assume people are evil, up to no good, or wrong until they prove otherwise. I prefer to give someone the benefit of the doubt, all while keeping a watchful and discerning eye.

None of this is meant to say we should trust everyone with everything. We must walk in wisdom and discerning of spirits as followers of Jesus Christ. If we don't, people we love, including ourselves, could be harmed.

We've had seasons where we missed it and seasons where we've been right on target. My prayer is to be on target more than I miss it. That is for the sake of not wanting to hurt others.

Maybe the next time you're falsely accused you could ask questions of your accuser to try to ascertain how they arrived at the false conclusion. Pray to be patient and kind. I know that's hard when you're being accused. Allow Holy Spirit to take control and the situation may just turn out for the good of all.

Godspeed as you do relationship with God and others!

Day 184

The Prophetess Huldah

2 Kings 22:3-23:30 / Acts 21:37-22:16 / Psalm 1 / Proverbs 18:11-12

Congratulations on making it halfway through the year as we read our Bibles together! We've completed the Psalms and are starting again. I wonder what new things we'll find as we read a second time. I'm excited to discover what Holy Spirit will place on my heart to talk about these next six months.

One topic that fascinates me is women in the Bible, along with women in leadership in general. Not every culture or belief system allows that women may lead in a spiritual capacity, but my husband and I fully agree with and support women in leadership. So, when I saw that there was a woman prophet named Huldah in 2 Kings 22:14, I wanted to try to find out a little more information about her.

In 2 Kings 22 (the only mention of her in scripture) she is referred to as "The Prophet Huldah." She lived about 624 BC and was married to a man named Shallum who was the keeper of the Temple wardrobe. They lived in the New Quarter of Jerusalem. That is all the information given in this text.

Huldah's name means "an earthling, a mole, weasel (a burrowing animal) or life." From my own observation, someone who burrows through the earth is one who is searching for treasure and truth.

The word used here for prophet or prophetess is "nebia" and it means "an inspired woman or a poetess." Her husband Shallum's name means "retribution", which is defined as "the dispensing or receiving of reward or punishment especially in the hereafter."

On further research for information on Huldah, history tells us she was a scholar and a seer (prophet) and was of high social ranking. Huldah was a woman of spiritual insight and intelligence. Her husband was also a trusted high-ranking person in society because one who had access to the king in an intimate relationship, such as his wardrobe manager, would have had private access others would not have had.

The New Quarter of Jerusalem, or second quadrant (Jerusalem was divided into four quadrants) was in the same section as the temple and the palace, further speaking to the high standing of this family.

In summary, it seems that Huldah was respected in both a worldly and a spiritual sense. It is interesting that King Josiah sent five of his male advisors to consult with her, so Josiah must have trusted in her reputation, judgment and ability to speak on the Lord's behalf.

I will leave you, as the reader, to draw your own conclusions regarding women in leadership positions. However, if you would like to study further, I want to recommend an excellent book to you. The Other Half of the Army by Phill Olson is filled with scripture that will lead you to some eye-opening conclusions!

May we, like Huldah, be of an excellent reputation, able to bear influence both in the world and in God's Kingdom!

Day 185

Listener or Talker?

2 Kings 23:31-25:30 / Acts 22:17-23:10 / Psalm 2 / Proverbs 18:13

Since I love to talk, I've had to work hard to become a better listener. I'm not saying I'm good at it, but I'm working to improve! In my excitement, I sometimes still interrupt or talk over top of others. I don't always listen well, because I'm trying to construct what I want to say next. However, I do earnestly love listening to someone else's story. People are fascinating because their experiences are so diverse.

So, when I read Proverbs 18:13, I was reminded yet again to continue working on being a good listener. The verse says this, "Spouting off before listening to the facts is both shameful and foolish."

If I'm not listening, when I have a chance to give input I may not answer in a relative manner. The question becomes, "Do I want to talk to be heard, or do I want to offer value to the one listening?"

There are times I'm afraid I'll forget what I was going to say. There are also times when it's better to simply listen, allowing the other person to process and come to their own conclusions. If I forget what I was going to say, maybe it didn't need to be said.

I've found that there are times input is valuable, and times when silence is what's best. I enjoy what I call verbal processing, meaning I learn as I speak. It's as if hearing the words out loud helps me come to a better conclusion. Some learn by asking good questions. Some learn by listening and pondering to themselves.

If you're a verbal processor, you know my pain. It's hard to be quiet! I'm also a kinesthetic learner, one who appreciates being hands-on, so being quiet and not actively participating in a discussion causes me to sometimes get lost in the conversation.

I like to use my hands and sometimes I get excited, and my volume goes up. However, when it comes to a proper response in the situation, working to curb my excitement will be to my benefit. If my excitement keeps me from listening well, I will not give input that is helpful.

Remember, the verse says speaking out of turn is "foolish and shameful." What do "foolish" and "shameful" mean? Let's find out by looking them up! For these two words, I'm looking at the Merriam Webster online dictionary.

"Foolish" means "lacking good sense, good judgment, or discretion." It can also mean "insignificant".

"Shameful", or "shame", means "a painful emotion caused by consciousness of guilt, shortcoming, or impropriety." And don't you feel that way when you've spoken out of turn or out of context?

I also think of Proverbs 17:28 which reads, "Even fools are thought wise when they keep silent; with their mouths shut, they seem intelligent."

And now we've come to a personal dilemma because like I said already, sometimes it is so hard to keep silent! Don't worry; difficulty in keeping silent doesn't make one a fool.

My son-in-law, Joshua, is excellent at observing and listening, then when he speaks, his words bring such wisdom and weight. There are times I wish I were more like Joshua. But then the Lord reminds me that He made each of us the way He did for a purpose. We can enjoy the quiet wisdom of a Joshua, and the exuberant input of our talkative friends.

I had a friend recently ask how she could become better at not interrupting. Before I answered, I had to laugh that she was asking me a question like that. But I do have some tips.

My first tip is to take notes as you listen, then if you have a response, you'll remember it. Second, take mental note that you do not always need to have a response. And third, don't listen with the intent of responding. If you forget your point or your response after you've listened well, perhaps the Lord would rather you not make the point.

Cheers to the talkers and cheers to the observers. We both have value, and I encourage you to keep being you!

Day 186

How Should I Treat My Enemies?

1 Chronicles 1:1-2:17 / Acts 23:11-35 / Psalm 3 / Proverbs 18:14-15

We've talked about enemies before, but I want to talk about them again. I'm not used to having enemies because I'm a kind, warm person and I work hard to forgive. When we offer someone forgiveness, it is for the health of our own souls, so if others choose to remain an enemy, that is upon their shoulders and not ours.

I used to say I had no enemies, but today the Lord had me look up the meaning of the word because sadly there are those who have made themselves enemies. The word "enemy" is defined as "a person who is actively opposed or hostile to someone." The Strong's Concordance also mentions an "adversary" which is defined as "one's opponent in a contest, conflict or dispute."

It hurts my heart to say that I have people who feel this way toward me. But I'm grateful to say that I have forgiven them, and I pray to continue to walk in forgiveness toward them. However, I have questions. When we're facing off against an enemy or adversary, where is God? What promises has He made to us? Psalm 3 speaks very well to this and offers some help and relief.

Verse 3 reads, "But you, O Lord, are a shield around me, you are my glory, the one who holds my head high." Verses 5-6 read, "I lay down and slept, yet I woke up in safety, for the Lord was watching over me. I am not afraid of ten thousand enemies who surround me on every side." And verse 7 reads, "Arise, O Lord! Rescue me, my God! Slap all my enemies in the face!"

That last line made me laugh! If the Lord is my shield, and my glory, and He lifts my head, I want to understand these words better.

The definition of the word "shield" is "a defense or protector, like the scales of a crocodile."

"Glory" is defined as "honor, dignity and reputation." I don't need to worry about my reputation because the Lord knows the truth!

The phrase "he lifts my head" means "He exalts or promotes me to high places; He holds me up and He sets me high." This sounds like a great vantage point to see everything around me!

These definitions are exciting enough all by themselves, but then we read that we don't have to be afraid even when ten thousand enemies are surrounding us. The protection of the Lord is astonishing in that He protects us simply because we belong to Him.

We didn't earn His protection; it appears to be a condition of our relationship. We have come under the protection of the King. If that doesn't make us confident and unafraid, I don't know what will!

It gives us courage to know that we're surrounded by the Lord and His Heavenly army. They are protecting us while also lifting us higher than any enemy. It's amazing that the God of the universe protects us.

So, it doesn't matter what the view of an enemy is on the subject. God's truth tells us we are protected and surrounded by Him. It is from this place we must approach life.

We must no longer approach our enemies from a heart of unforgiveness, bitterness, or anger. We must continue to forgive them every time something happens, and then we will live in peace and safety!

Day 187

When Angry, Wait

1 Chronicles 2:18-4:4 / Acts 24 / Psalm 4 / Proverbs 18:16-18

I want to talk to you about anger. I bring this subject up again because as you've read, it used to be a big issue for me. Thankfully I've learned to process anger better and that has helped me grow in this area. I still get angry sometimes, but nothing like I used to.

As I've learned to be led by Holy Spirit, it has become easier to recognize anger's trap. I'm not saying the process through anger is easy, but I've come to realize that anger solves absolutely nothing. Anger also causes me to feel horrible physically and emotionally.

> "Don't sin by letting anger control you. Think about it overnight and remain silent. Interlude." —Psalm 4:4

In reading this verse I noticed that anger is not sin. The sin is in letting anger control us. The word "anger" in this verse is quite descriptive in the original language. It means "tremble, quake, rage, quiver, be agitated, be excited, be perturbed, be disquieted."

I believe this verse is referring to anything that unsettles us without us resolving the issue. It's not a sin to feel this way; it is a sin to allow it to control our actions, thoughts and feelings. The word "sin" is also interesting.

In Hebrew it means "offended, blame, fault, miss the way, go wrong, to induce to sin, to cause to sin." I love that the verse tells us to think about it overnight and remain silent. "To remain silent" means "to wait or to be still."

Who out there wants to immediately rant and rave when some-one has made you angry? I get it. I'm the same way! But wisdom seems to be dictating that we close our mouths (except to pray, which is an important part of working through something that has unset-tled us) and wait. What are we waiting for?

I believe we're waiting for our hearts and minds to calm down, and we're waiting for God's instructions on how to handle the situa-tion. I promise He will not tell us to blast the other person, or to try to get them back for what they did.

If Jesus prayed from the cross for His Father to forgive those who were putting Him to death, I'm positive we can forgive anyone for what they've done. I do understand that some horrific things have happened to some of us, and forgiveness can seem impossible.

It might take some time, and it may take more than one for-giveness session, but we are able to overcome this as Holy Spirit empowers us! Remember it is for our freedom that we forgive. The other person may never understand what they did and that is not our concern. Our concern is our own heart.

The word "interlude", or "Selah", is defined as "a technical mu-sical term probably showing accentuation, pause, or interruption." So, after you've been quiet overnight, then wait some more. At least that's what I'm reading, and I think waiting twice is a good idea!

My advice when you're angry, and God's Word seems to agree, is to wait, pray, wait, forgive. Hopefully that will keep us out of trouble!

Day 188

He's Got You Surrounded

1 Chronicles 4:5-5:17 / Acts 25 / Psalm 5 / Proverbs 18:19

Have you ever felt surrounded and not in a good way? Maybe it was a group of friends teasing you, or maybe it was something unseen that you couldn't quite explain but you felt fearful. Yes, the air surrounds us in the natural world. But we are also surrounded by the spiritual world, even if we can't see what's there.

I guess it might seem kind of creepy to be surrounded by things and beings we can't see. I can understand that. There are times I'm walking through my house at night, and I feel a presence that disturbs my spirit. It is then I begin to pray because those unseen "scaries" are not allowed in my space!

We are also surrounded by the Lord. As I considered the word "surround", several verses came to mind. The first was from our reading today in Psalm 5:12 and it says,

"For you bless the godly, O LORD;
You surround them with Your shield of love."

Most of the time a shield is for front defense only, but God's "love shield" surrounds us, protecting even our backs! What else surrounds us? Psalm 32:7 NASB says,

"You are my hiding place; You keep me from trouble; You surround me with songs of deliverance. Selah."

Songs of deliverance are songs that declare my freedom! This is getting exciting! Let's look at what else surrounds us.

"Many are the sorrows of the wicked, but he who trusts in the LORD, lovingkindness shall surround him."—Psalm 32:10

"As the mountains surround Jerusalem, so the LORD surrounds His people from this time forth and forever."—Psalm 125:2

There may be a few more, but these are amazing and encouraging! To recap with what and Who surrounds us:

His shield of love
Songs of freedom
Lovingkindness
The Lord.

Do you feel protected and safe? I sure do! The next time you feel surrounded by evil, or by someone taunting you, or whatever attempts to put fear or intimidation upon you, remember the four things above.

I believe as the Lord surrounds us, His presence far surpasses any other thing that would attempt to surround us! Rest secure in Him. Do not fear what man or the unseen world can do to you, because you are surrounded and protected by the LORD Himself!

Day 189

Share Your Story

1 Chronicles 5:18-6:81 / Acts 26 / Psalm 6 / Proverbs 18:20-21

Our stories matter. The highs and lows, the triumphs and trag-edies, are all a valuable part of the events that shape who we are and who we are becoming. Some distain trials, but the truth is everyone faces them and if we look at them properly, we'll understand that trials teach us, causing maturity and growth. I encourage you to share your story whenever you have the opportunity.

When we share our stories, some details need to be kept private, but even those most private details may have value to someone who is facing the same thing. We must allow Holy Spirit to lead, and we must be willing to be vulnerable with His leading.

I don't recommend wholesale sharing of all our dirt because that is not wise. However, once you have gone through something, you are able to reach a hand back and help the next person.

2 Corinthians 1:3-4 tells us,

"All praise to God, the Father of our Lord Jesus Christ. God is our merciful Father and the source of all comfort. He comforts us in all our troubles so that we can comfort others. When they are troubled, we will be able to give them the same comfort God has given us."

God comforts us so we can comfort others. Our lives are meant to be shared with one another. That's what struck me in today's read-ing in Acts 26. Paul is recounting his story of having persecuted the

Church, then having been interrupted by Jesus Christ and called to something new.

Paul had been in prison for a few years by this time and he is telling his story to King Agrippa of Judea (the Greek word for Judah), and his wife Bernice, along with Festus the Roman governor, also in Judea.

As Paul shares his testimony, I'm reminded of the fact that no one can refute our experience. They may not believe what has happened to us, but if we are in front of a compassionate listener, they should affirm what we've experienced.

When we share the Gospel of the kingdom, our personal story is an important part. As a matter of fact, when Paul was sharing his story, King Agrippa was very receptive and it appears as if he was feeling conviction of the Holy Spirit, because he said to Paul, "Do you think you can persuade me to become a Christian so quickly?"

I believe that is exactly what Paul was hoping for! Even though he was a prisoner, he was intent on fulfilling his calling to bring many to faith through Jesus Christ. He was unashamed of what Jesus had done for him since knocking him off his horse and revealing the truth to him.

Our story of faith is valuable to us and others, but all the other stories of our lives are also valuable, so I encourage you to be courageous and share when prompted.

Sharing your story is part of your growth journey, so please share when you sense an open door. You never know how much this will impact both you and those listening.

Day 190

Wives, We Are a Treasure

1 Chronicles 7-8 / Acts 27:1-20 / Psalm 7 / Proverbs 18:22

Marriage is valued by God, and yes, marriage is a traditional covenant between a man and a woman with God as the sealer of that covenant. God created man, then he created woman from man. God knew man needed a helper, a partner, someone to walk with him. I believe God also knew that we women needed the same.

I have compassion for my single friends who wish to be married. We are not meant to be alone. We are meant to live in a community. And while I know my single friends are thankful for their families and friends, I join my prayers with theirs for that longed-for mate!

Ladies who are blessed to be a wife, did you know the Bible says you are a treasure to your husband? Yes, it's true. Proverbs 18:22 tells us, "The man who finds a wife finds a treasure, and he receives favor from the Lord." Not only are we a treasure, because of us our husbands receive favor from the Lord.

I plan to live 120 years, and I realize many of my friends don't see life this way. They don't want to be "old" and still living on earth. I happen to want to be here for as long as the Lord allows so I may continue to bring the "song" of my life into the earth. Then I will happily move my residence to Heaven when God says it's time!

If I'm going to live to 120, I've told Jeff he must do the same. After all, I want my best friend to enjoy long life with me.

Whether this is God's plan or not, I plan to live an abundant life and to enjoy every minute with the blessing God gave me in Jeff.

I need to remind him that I'm a treasure and I bring him favor. Won't that be fun to do!

In our home, as well as our home church, we believe that women are co-equal with men. God says so in His Word! There is not time for a full study or proof here, but I can recommend some reading material and some scriptures if you want to explore this further.

Suffice it to say that in all of scripture there were women in leadership alongside men. One is not of more value than the other.

If I'm a treasure to my husband and bring him favor, what do I get out of the union? I'm sure there are many answers to this question, but one I'd like to mention is the safety and security that comes from my husband being submitted to God and loving me as Christ loves His Church. That is a powerful love!

So, wives, when your husband comes home tonight, let's have a little fun with him. You should tell him that you are his treasure and that he has favor because of you. I'm sure there may be mixed reactions such as raised eyebrows, smiles, laughs, and quizzical looks. But I bet some of you will receive affirmation and hugs. I know that's what I'll receive!

Day 191

Listen to the "Know-it-all"

1 Chronicles 9-10 / Acts 27:21-44 / Psalm 8 / Proverbs 18:23-24

When I was younger, I thought I knew everything. I was too wise in my own eyes. Now that I'm older, even though I have more wisdom and knowledge, I feel I have so much to learn. Then I was not as inclined to take advice or counsel from anyone, now I want to find those wise friends who know me and my situation and ask for their input when I need to make important decisions. The person I ask advice from the most is my husband, Jeff.

In reading about Paul and the shipwreck in Acts 27, I noticed something. A centurion guarding Paul, along with both the pilot and owner of the ship, were not willing to listen to Paul's warning about impending disaster on the voyage. Paul had no choice but to allow events to unfold. And sure enough, as Paul knew from the Spirit, the ship ended up in trouble.

The next warning that Paul gave, however, was heeded by the commanding officer and soldiers. Paul assured everyone that they would all be saved, but that the sailors were required to remain on board, and they needed to disembark together. Thankfully they listened and did what Paul said. It seems that since his first warning about the storm was ignored and turned out to be accurate, they didn't want to take a chance with his second warning.

How often do we listen to someone the first time they try to tell us something? Are we willing to listen to someone whose reputation has not been proven to us? **I believe that no matter how long we've known someone, we should take in the information they are shar-**

ing, then pray that Holy Spirit will confirm in our hearts if this is the right direction or response for us.

It certainly will not hurt us to at least listen and consider the possibility that what we're hearing is correct and may be helpful. Therefore, it's important to be humble and teachable. Some don't like to feel there is something they don't know or something they "missed," but none of us can know all things. That's why we need one another.

Even if you're faced with a "know-it-all," there may be value in what is being said. I'll admit, it's difficult not to ignore this type of person, but if a donkey can speak as one did in Numbers 22:28, then we can learn something valuable from anyone, even the most disagreeable person!

So, be teachable, be humble, be willing to listen and consider and you may just find yourself saved from disaster!

Day 192

The Richness of Friendship

1 Chronicles 11:1-12:18 / Acts 28 / Psalm 9:1-12 / Proverbs 19:1-3

I've had many friends over my lifetime. There are some from childhood that I am still connected with, but I rarely see them. I have friends all around the world, as well as all over the United States. I've lost friends. I've made new friends. Most of the time friendships are a treasure and a blessing, but there are times when a misunderstanding must be worked out – when forgiveness must be offered and received.

Imagine how David felt in 1 Chronicles chapters 11-12 as he was being crowned king of all Israel after Saul's death. He had been hiding from King Saul for nearly seven years. During that time, he lost and gained friends as well as family relationships. He even had men who were from Saul's own family who came to him while in hiding and pledged allegiance to him. I'm sure that made Saul happy, not!

I love the stories of David's thirty mighty men, including the three who were his top warriors. They were brave, fearless, courageous and any other mighty word we could find to describe them. But what I appreciate the most is that his men were loyal. They came to David in a time of great need, and they vowed to stand by him.

"Amasai, the leader of the Thirty, said to David on behalf of all the men, 'We are yours, David! We are on your side, son of Jesse. Peace and prosperity be with you, and success to all who help you, for your God is the one who helps you.'" — 1 Chronicles 12:18

Who wouldn't want a friend like that! I have something I say to my family and friends, and I've even said this to God. "I am yours and you are mine." This is not said in some weird ownership way. It is said in a way that says I am willing to give my time, talent, treasure and heart to them. I'm also excited for the rewards of the two-way friendships.

We all have those in our lives who only "take" from us, and that is not easy to understand. When you're a giver, it's hard to imagine someone giving to you on a continual basis without your own heart being moved to give in return. Therefore, those who are only takers may end up not receiving as much of our time. All of us want to be around those who give back and who speak life in return for the life we are giving and speaking over them.

Friendship is hard work, but the rewards are worth every minute spent sowing into the lives of others. Proverbs 11:25 says this,

> "The generous will prosper; those who refresh others
> will themselves be refreshed."

That is a wonderful promise and a good reason to reach out in kindness to others.

If you're fortunate enough to be in a circle of friends who love to give to each other, you know what I mean. It's as if they fight one another to see who can give first or give most! It's funny, but sometimes people must tell me that what they are giving is a gift, so that I may thank them and stop myself from reciprocating.

That is the kind of person we all want on the other end of our giving – one with whom it becomes like a competition to see who can outgive the other! I think life is richer when we live that way. It can also get to be comical, because at some point one forgets who gave first and the giving is a never-ending, beautiful story.

That's how it is with Jesus. We love Him, but He loved us first. We give our lives to Him, but He gave His life first. Malachi 3:9-10 speaks about tithing, but I believe it could apply to all giving. It says in verse 11,

> "Test me in this... and see if I will not throw open
> the floodgates of Heaven and pour out so much blessing
> that there will not be room enough to store it."

I believe God wants us to test Him as we give in every area because He wants to pour out blessings. No matter what you give in His Name, He will always give an abundance back to you. You simply cannot give more than God can give!

So, love your friends. Give them your life along with everything that's in your heart to give, and watch your circle expand to be so large that you are awed by how rich you are. I am that rich. And I believe God has only just begun to bless me! I know He has surprises around every corner for me and for you.

Day 193

I Am Yours; You Are Mine

1 Chronicles 12:19-14:17 / Romans 1:1-17
Psalm 9:13-20 / Proverbs 19:4-5

I wrote yesterday about friendship, and in that entry, I talked about "givers" and "takers". I assert we must be both, maybe not at the same moment in time, but as an overall picture we cannot be only one or the other or we will be out of balance.

If we're all "giving", we will be empty. And if we're all "taking" we will also be empty. You may disagree with that but if the richness is in giving, we are empty if we choose not to do so.

In Romans 1 Paul is excited to visit the Christians in Rome both because he wants to "bring some spiritual gift that will help (them) grow strong in the Lord" and because He "also wants to be encouraged by yours (faith)."

I love that the Apostle Paul does not think so highly of himself that he believes he is the only one who can give spiritual food and that he cannot also receive from those he wants to encourage. That's the way it should be! And that is part of the deficit in some churches who believe only those in leadership have something to give.

We are all ministers of God's grace, and we must always be willing to share our gifts with everyone in the body of Christ, even with our leaders. Both leaders and learners have need of one another. Never let the congregant believe she or he has nothing to give.

You have been given the same eternal life, the same Holy Spirit, the same opportunity to "bring some spiritual gift" as your leaders. Your role in the body may differ, but your value does not.

Your leader needs you! We all need the strength, teaching and encouragement from those we have been blessed to have around us. Remember, it is God who brought us together because He knows we will bring value to one another's lives!

If you're the one who is hesitant to speak up, may I encourage you to prayerfully offer your gift to the body? When I say, "speak up", I'm not referring only to those with gifts as speakers. What about the ones who speak by serving quietly? However, I've found that it's the quiet ones who often have the deepest treasure that comes forth when they do speak!

My son-in-law is reserved and quiet, but when he speaks, he brings wisdom from his many years of observing and learning. Maybe we should find that quiet friend and ask what they are thinking. I bet we'll find great wealth there!

If you're one who finds it hard to receive, pray to let that go! I am preaching to myself here because I've had to work at being a better receiver. The thing that helped me most was to realize that my refusal to receive is robbing the giver of a blessing. If I'm wanting to bless others, that must include being willing to receive from them!

When you gather with other believers, and I'm assuming you do, be prepared to give and to receive. Hebrews 10:25 tells us, "And let us not neglect our meeting together, as some people do, but encourage one another, especially now that the day of his return is drawing near."

It's a brave thing indeed to bring one's heart to give away to others because you may find your heart broken at times. But the Lord tells us simply to give. When you gather with your spiritual family, what gift will you take with you? I encourage you not to limit yourself to one or two possibilities. Ask the Lord what He would have you give. You may be surprised to hear Him tell you to give something you've never given before!

Day 194

The "Value" of Idols?

1 Chronicles 15:1-16:36 / Romans 1:18-32
Psalm 10:1-15 / Proverbs 19:6-7

When you hear the word "idols" what is your first thought? Do you think of actual statues made of stone or wood? Or do you think of anything that we place ahead of God in our affection?

Both are true.

Here is the dictionary definition of the word *idol*: "an image or representation of a god used as an object of worship."

And another definition is: "a person or thing that is greatly admired, loved, or revered."

Most Christians would probably say they don't have wood or stone figures in their homes that they worship – unless they are unaware of the history of some of the artifacts they've collected. However, all of us struggle with placing things, thoughts, feelings, etc. ahead of and above our affection for God.

All through the Old Testament idols are mentioned many times. And almost every time I read about a wooden or stone statue, I think about how absurd it is that anyone would worship a created object and call that a god.

Wouldn't God have been the One who did the creating? What can a statue do? Nothing. It can neither speak nor hear so there is no help offered when you're in need.

The past two days I've come across a couple of verses that show the futility of holding these objects in high regard. Here are a couple of examples of the spiritual value of these items.

1 Chronicles 14:12, "The Philistines had abandoned their gods there, and David gave orders to burn them in the fire." I know I shouldn't laugh, but this is funny to me. If your god can be burned in a fire, it's not a god.

"The gods of other nations are mere idols,
but the LORD made the Heavens!"—1 Chronicles 16:26

"And instead of worshiping the glorious, ever-living God, they worshiped idols made to look like mere people and birds and animals and reptiles."—Romans 1:23

The Philistines abandoned their gods. That means their gods depend on men to carry them. And then they allowed themselves to be burned. Hmmm... that doesn't sound like a god who could help me with anything!

In the phrase, "The gods of other nations are mere idols," the Hebrew word for "idols" is "elil" which means "good for nothing or worthless." Again, what can these do to help me when I am in need?

And finally, why would anyone worship what has been created, such as people, birds, animals, or reptiles? Would that person not consider that the Creator would be greater than the thing that was created?

The answer is that deception does not allow these thinkers to see that God is the Creator and the One to be worshiped instead of the things that He created being worshiped. Their eyes are blind, their ears are deaf, and their understanding is darkened by the enemy. Mere logic will not allow one to understand truth; only God's Spirit can reveal truth and open our ability to see and hear.

As for the things we place ahead of God – the opinions of others, our hurts and struggles, our views of Him that don't match His true character – these are unseen idols that also need to be addressed. Maybe it's easier to rid ourselves of things that are seen. It is the unseen idols of the heart that are harder to discover and remove. But God is with us to enable us to do just that!

When you find yourself thinking in a way contrary to God and His Word, you have an idol to remove. And once removed, you must replace that idolatrous thinking with His truth. Never leave an empty hole because something will attempt to fill it.

Today, I pray you can identify at least one area that needs to be uprooted and replaced both with God's truth and His Spirit. May you have grace to remove some idols and walk in freedom!

Day 195

His Kindness Overcomes Chaos

1 Chronicles 16:37-18:17 / Romans 2:1-24
Psalm 10:16-18 / Proverbs 19:8-9

The goodness and kindness of God, although undeserved by all of us, is poured out on every single person on earth. This kindness is poured out whether we are aware of it, and whether we receive and are thankful for it. Breath, health, peace, provision, rain, friendships – all of these are evidence of God's blessing upon us. Once we are aware of His kindness, how many of us give Him the thanks He deserves?

Twice in my reading today I noticed the writer giving thanks for God's kindness and promises. In 1 Chronicles 17:16-27, David is praying and thanking God for the promised legacy given in and through his family. And in Romans 1:4, Paul reminds us that God's kindness is intended to turn us from our sin.

I've said it before and I'll say it again; God is not an angry God waiting to destroy us when we do something wrong! He loves us in our mess and in our sin. How could He not?

For one, we are all still wrestling through sin and imperfection. And secondly, Jesus Christ paid the penalty for our sin, so now we are the very righteousness of God through Him.

Are we aware of how blessed and rich we are? I understand that all of us face trials – sickness, loss, relational difficulty, etc. but that does not mean we are not blessed. It simply means we are living on planet earth. Every single person faces difficulty, and every single person faces blessing. Some difficulty may seem worse than others, but God has given us grace to walk through that dark place.

And some may appear to be more blessed than others but remember that with blessing comes responsibility. Some may welcome the weight of blessing with responsibility, and some may be thankful to lead a quiet life.

"When someone has been given much, much will be required in return." —Luke 12:48.

I can't move on from the topic of trials without acknowledging there are terrible injustices in the world. Some live with unbearable circumstances through no fault of their own – suffering horrible things no one should ever have to suffer. It is for those we pray for justice and freedom.

There is a very real evil force that affects the earth and causes all kinds of chaos. Thankfully, that evil will be destroyed one day because of what Jesus Christ did on the cross. Someone will be thrown into the Lake of Fire.

If you find yourself in a hard circumstance, or a difficult trial, I encourage you to pray and ask God for help. Ask Him to reveal a blessing to you, or a truth, or a promise, or something that you can hold onto during your suffering. It is in those dark seasons we most need an anchor to hold onto.

Our greatest anchor is, of course, Jesus Christ. He stills our soul when chaos comes. And He promised never to leave us.

"So be strong and courageous! Do not be afraid and do not panic before them. For the Lord your God will personally go ahead of you. He will neither fail you nor abandon you."—Deuteronomy 31:6

Please take that to heart today!

Day 196

Who to Take with You into A Fight

1 Chronicles 19-21 / Romans 2:25-3:8/ Psalm 11 / Proverbs 19:10-12

If you're like me, you don't want to go into a fight, disagreement, or scary situation alone. Maybe there are some who say they are fine standing up to a bully by themselves, but I prefer to have a buddy along – someone who is on my side, and someone who knows, loves, and will protect me!

The Old Testament kings were always at war with someone. For one, they were at war with God's people because they were inhabiting the land God had given to Israel's descendants. The kings who had lived in the nations God gave to His people had also been at war for years, trying to gain dominance, power, and wealth.

King David was one such man who was at war most of his adult life. Some nation or another was either plotting an attack, forming an alliance against, or attacking God's people. Thankfully, God was on His people's side!

But David made a mistake; the scripture says he sinned. In 1 Chronicles 21, David decided to take a census of his fighting men. Why was this a sin? I believe it was because David was taking note of his human resources by counting how many men he had who were ready to go into battle.

Repeatedly, God answered His people's prayers and delivered them from the nations around them, and it didn't make any difference who had more men in the battle. When the Lord is on your side and He has told you to fight, He intends to fight alongside you and bring a victory.

There was no need for David to assess his own strength because God had proven Himself to be strongly on David's side many times. Maybe it was offensive to God that David would depend on himself instead of depending on God. How many times have we done the same thing?

We prove we are not depending on God when we don't go to Him first, asking for help. We prove we are relying on our own strength when we barrel ahead at the first sign of trouble. Even if there is an emergency that requires immediate attention, pray as you go or act. God will show up and give clarity, help and healing in the situation.

The way I see it we have three options for whom to depend on in a tough situation. We can depend on ourselves and our own wisdom and strength, we can depend on our family and friends, or we can depend on God. Even when we choose to depend on God, we'll have to take some course of action. And sometimes that action is to follow these words:

"Stand still and see My salvation!"

Standing still is an action. Prayer is also an action.

Day 197

Christian, what is Your Work?

1 Chronicles 22-23 / Romans 3:9-31/ Psalm 12 / Proverbs 19:13-14

Most of us want to do the right thing. We want to please our parents when we're children, although some of us can be mischievous! We want to please our families, our bosses, those we go to church with, and most of all we want to please God.

Some do the right thing because someone might be watching. Some do the right thing because they think it will earn them favor. Others do the right thing simply because they know it's right.

I really enjoyed reading Romans 3:19-31 today. There are those who believe when they keep God's law, they become righteous. But verse 20 tells us God's intended purpose for bringing the law; the law simply shows us how sinful we are.

Once the law has done its work in showing us our sin, what are we to do? Are we to be left feeling lost and without an answer to our sinful hearts? Thankfully, no! Verse 22 tells us we are made right with God by placing our faith in Jesus Christ. And this is true for everyone who believes in Him.

The answer to our sin and guilt problem is an easy answer to find, but it's hard for some to believe. Faith in Jesus Christ is the answer to our sin problem. Our works, or the good things we do, will not save us from God's judgment. If you want to get away from the judgment of God, you must hide yourself in Jesus Christ by believing He is the Son of God who came to reconcile you in relationship with His Father.

It is Holy Spirit that draws us into faith, yet some still believe we must work to keep the gift of salvation God gave us through His Son Jesus Christ. We don't work to earn our salvation, and neither must we work to keep it.

Yes, there is still work we may accomplish and be proud of! There is nothing wrong with working hard and drawing satisfaction from that. As a matter of fact, our hard, diligent work blesses God and allows others to see His character in us. It is only the area of salvation that we may take no credit for. Jesus Christ deserves all credit for the provision and keeping of our salvation.

Philippians 2:12b says, "Work hard to show the results of your salvation, obeying God with deep reverence and fear." In this verse, our "work" is our obedience.

Here is what John 6:29 says about our work, "Jesus told them, 'This is the only work God wants from you: Believe in the One He has sent.'" This verse says our "work" is to believe in Jesus Christ.

Do you want to do work for God? Then obey Him and believe in Jesus Christ. I'm reminded of an old hymn "Trust and Obey." Here are some of those lyrics.

"When we walk with the Lord,
in the light of His Word,
what a glory He sheds on our way.
While we do His good will,
He abides with us still,
and with all who will trust and obey.
Trust and obey for there's no other way
to be happy in Jesus, but to trust and obey."

Trust Him. Obey Him. Believe Him. Our "work" for Him is simple, but it will take determination and our own personal diligence to accomplish this work!

Day 198

I'm Working through My Trust Issues

1 Chronicles 24:1-26:11 / Romans 4:1-12/ Psalm 13 / Proverbs 19:15-16

My counselor used to tell me I had trust issues. This was after a year of meeting with her, and it seemed that every time we came up against a thought pattern that needed correction and healing, it was connected to lack of trust. That comes from being hurt and disappointed by people.

At some point I began to wonder if I would ever trust people again. I've been forgiving everyone I can think of every time something happens, and I wonder if the list will ever end. Every time something new arises, I forgive that also, even if it's the same person and for the one hundredth time!

As I shared part of my story with a friend, and I keep the details very limited because part of my healing process is not rehashing the past, she looked at me and said, "No wonder you have trust issues!" Hmm. I'm sure I'm not the only one who has experienced betrayal and relational pain though.

There have been a handful of friends over the past few years who have been with me through it all, and those are the ones I trust and feel safe with. Thankfully, I feel safe with my "five family" (that's what I call Jeff, our children and myself). But new friendships take me awhile because it's exhausting building something when you're not sure what will happen.

All that said, there is One I trust and feel safe with and that is my God. Psalm 13:5-6 says:

"But I trust in Your unfailing love. I will rejoice
because You have rescued me. I will sing to the LORD
because He is good to me."

God has always been good to me, even when bad things have happened. He doesn't stop all the bad, but He is with us in all the bad. He is also a covering for the blows. I believe that because we're in Christ, the blows hit Him first. Anything that comes our way has first come through Him. Imagine how difficult it would be if things hit us straight on.

I'm thankful for God's protection and care. I'm thankful He's always with us. I'm thankful He covers us. I can't imagine life without Him. He is in us, through us and for us. He fights on our behalf, giving us wisdom and strength to walk through the inevitable battles that will come. And the battles will come.

I wish I could tell you that you'll have no battles, because they are painful. But then I would be condemning you to a weak life because you would never be trained for war. Make no mistake, we are in a spiritual war. If we don't go through hard things, we will not learn, grow, or become strong.

The devil is attempting to take away our very lives, along with everything that is dear to us. But the good news is, he has lost already! Because of what Jesus Christ accomplished on the cross in purchasing our forgiveness, salvation, healing, deliverance, freedom, and everything else we will ever need in this life and the next, we are more than conquerors through Him!

Even when it looks like our lives are being ruined, if we're in Christ, we are winning! I know it seems crazy, but it's true! Look at the back of the book – the end of the story – it says WE WIN! We win because Jesus Christ has won and because we are His.

End. Of. Story.

Day 199

The Gatekeepers

1 Chronicles 26:12-27:34 / Romans 4:13-5:5/ Psalm 14 / Proverbs 19:17

Everyone wants to protect their family as well as their property. Whether you choose security systems, a guard dog, to be trained in the proper use of firearms, etc., everyone has some type of security in mind. It's sad to think that there are people out there who would want to invade, harm, or steal from others, but sadly this is the world we live in.

As I've read through the Old Testament, I've seen many verses that speak about gatekeepers at the temple. At first, I thought it odd that a temple would need gatekeepers. I mean, who is going to do harm in the house of God? But then I considered that the descendants of Israel were surrounded by enemy nations, wild animals, and the same types of evil we are still surrounded by today.

1 Chronicles 26:12-13 says,

"These divisions of the gatekeepers were named for their family leaders, and like the other Levites, they served at the house of the LORD. They were assigned by families for guard duty at the various gates, without regard to age or training, for it was all decided by means of sacred lots."

There are lots of details regarding which families oversaw each of the gates on the north, south, east, and west side of the temple. There was also a need to guard the storehouse, the gateway to the temple, the gateway to the courtyard, etc.

I think when we're reading scripture, we tend to forget their times were just like ours regarding safety and protection of property and persons. Even today, many churches have armed security teams. Most visitors would not know that but there is a well-oiled security plan in place due to all the shootings and violence we face today.

This causes me to think about another need we have in the body of Christ and that is for spiritual guards, or watchmen. We're sometimes aware of physical threats, but what about spiritual threats? What about the threats we can't see? As I've written before, the LORD has been teaching me about guarding and praying over my territory.

Since we have a church in our home, we have many people coming in and out, and those people bring in with them whatever spirits are attached to their lives. Those spirits could affect our family, the people who are here, and the atmosphere in our territory.

I regularly pray for removal of "enemy entities," for muzzling of these entities as people come and go, and for opportunities for freedom from these influences as people are ready. The church doesn't speak much about demonic deliverance, but the enemy is still seeking whom he may devour. The Bible tells us the enemy is seeking also to steal, kill and destroy in our lives.

We must not forget his schemes. We must be on the alert. We must discern the spirits that are affecting those we fellowship with and pray for opportunities for them to be free from these spirits, and filled with God's Spirit instead.

Demonic deliverance doesn't need to be scary or loud or "showy." We have authority in Christ to speak to these powerless entities, telling them to leave, and sending them to be judged at the foot of the cross, or to go into dark places.

Once our family and friends are free from an evil spirit, we must always pray that the once-occupied place in their soul will be filled with Holy Spirit. Then Holy Spirit will complete His healing and restoring work.

Do not be fearful of praying over someone to deliver them from evil! Be bold, courageous gatekeepers and watchmen in your territory! The Spirit of the living God is within you!

Day 200

Our Intimate God

1 Chronicles 28-29 / Romans 5:6-21/ Psalm 15 / Proverbs 19:18-19

I've heard the argument that the Old Testament portrays God as angry, hard, and lacking in desire for intimate relationship with His people. It is true that there were only a few who God spoke with on an intimate level, at least from what we have recorded in scripture. There are likely many stories of which we are unaware.

In reading scripture, I have read several stories of intimate relationship between God and men like Abram, Moses, Jacob (Israel), King David, and several others. As I read in 1 Chronicles 28, it seems as if David is encouraging his son to have the same intimate relationship with God that he has enjoyed. Let's read verse 9 together, then I want to study some of the wording because I believe we'll find friendship with God at the center of this verse.

"And Solomon, my son, learn to know the God of your ancestors intimately. Worship and serve Him with your whole heart and a willing mind. For the LORD sees every heart and knows every plan and thought. If you seek him, you will find him. But if you forsake Him, He will reject you forever."—1 Chronicles 28:9

Let's define a few of the words from this verse for better understanding. The word "intimately" means "to know by experience, to see and understand." The phrase "whole heart" means "especially friendly, at peace, safe." A "willing mind" is defined as "pleased with, delight in, desire, favor." Finally, the phrase, "If you seek Him, you will find Him" means "to be encountered, to be discovered."

This does not sound like a distant and angry relationship to me. Words such as "peace", "safe", and "pleased with" all sound like words one might use to describe a close friend. God is not hiding from us, making sure we never encounter His presence or understand His heart. He wants us to find and know Him.

As a matter of fact, I believe He is as excited about a relationship with us as we are with Him. Imagine the God Who created everything wanting to spend time with little ol' me and you!

He does want to spend time with us. He doesn't want to spend time out of duty either; He loves our times together. I hope you enjoy His friendship in the same way.

Let me encourage you to find a quiet space and to sit with Him for a bit. Whether you have ten minutes or an hour, I promise you'll come to enjoy your time together. He will speak to you, share pictures with you, tell you about your future, and most of all He'll tell you how much you're loved!

Day 201

Every Good Thing Comes from Him

2 Chronicles 1-3 / Romans 6 / Psalm 16 / Proverbs 19:20-21

In 1998 I was surprised to learn that a longtime family friend wanted Jeff and me to execute her will and estate. What I didn't know when I signed the paperwork was that she was dying and would be with the Lord about 2 weeks later. She asked me to bring to the hospital all her earrings for her to choose a pair to wear. I didn't know how little time she had left.

After Myra passed, we were further surprised to learn as stated in her will, she had left us everything she owned. I guess that's why her lawyer was with her that day we visited the hospital. As her lawyer read to us her wishes after her passing, we realized that we had been named sole heirs of her insurance, her retirement, her home and all its contents – everything. To say we were shocked is an understatement.

As we sorted through everything in her home, preparing to empty the house so we could sell it, we made some beautiful walks down memory lane. Myra had been a congregant in the church my dad pastored for eight years. After the church closed, and my parents moved to North Carolina, Myra still called me to talk and ask me to pray for her. I suppose my love and care blessed her.

As I read Psalm 16 today, there were several verses that stood out to me. Verse 2 reads, "I said to the LORD, 'You are my Master! Every good thing I have comes from you.'"

Verses 5-6 read, "LORD, you alone are my inheritance, my cup of blessing. You guard all that is mine. The land you have given me is a pleasant land. What a wonderful inheritance!"

Did Myra leave us her possessions because she loved me? Or had the LORD wanted to bless my family to help us fulfill His word to us? I believe it was both!

A couple of years prior to us receiving this inheritance, Jeff came home from work one day telling me he had heard God tell him we needed to be out of debt within five years. If my hubby comes home with direction from the Lord, I'm all in!

So, we began attacking the principle on our mortgage every time he got a bonus at his job in the car business. Jeff was good at his job and God blessed us. With the addition of the money Myra left us, the house was paid off in less than the five-year deadline.

Every good thing comes from Him.
He guards all that is mine.
What a wonderful inheritance we have!

We have had several stories of God speaking to us, then providing the resources as we obeyed His word. God has faithfully led us every step of the way, even in the steps where we could not see His feet.

There are times I don't understand His goodness to me. There are times I don't feel I deserve His love. Yet there He is every moment blessing my family and me with Himself.

He is doing the same thing for you! It's just a matter of opening your eyes and your heart so you can see and comprehend His blessings. One of the songs I enjoy has a line that says, "His goodness is running after, it's running after me!" I believe He chases us down with blessings because He loves us more than words.

Quick! Look behind you! There He is again, chasing you down to bless you!

Day 202

The Beauty of His Presence

2 Chronicles 4:1-6:11 / Romans 7:1-13 / Psalm 17 / Proverbs 19:22-23

I really enjoy singing and worshiping. If I wasn't such a lover of God's Word, I might say the singing is my favorite part. Honestly, it's hard to choose between the two, so I won't. I will instead choose Jesus. I choose His presence, Himself, and His revelation of Himself to me.

As I read 2 Chronicles 5:12-14, I was trying to imagine the scene. What did the musicians look like? What did the music sound like? And when the glorious presence of the LORD filled the temple, what would it have been like to be there? I wish I could have been in attendance!

Here are the verses so you can also imagine:

"And the Levites who were musicians—Asaph, Heman, Jeduthun, and all their sons and brothers—were dressed in fine linen robes and stood at the east side of the altar playing cymbals, lyres, and harps. They were joined by 120 priests who were playing trumpets. The trumpeters and singers performed together in unison to praise and give thanks to the Lord. Accompanied by trumpets, cymbals, and other instruments, they raised their voices and praised the Lord with these words: 'He is good! His faithful love endures forever!' At that moment a thick cloud filled the Temple of the Lord. The priests could not continue their service because of the cloud, for the glorious presence of the Lord filled the Temple of God."

The music from the middle east does not sound like our music in the west. Our hymns, our modern worship songs and our choruses are not the same in lyrics or in sound. When we're in Heaven we'll be able to experience the music and beauty of the cultures from all the nations. I can't wait to hear that! Since every tongue, tribe, and nation will be in Heaven, we will get to know our brothers and sisters in a much deeper way.

I'm now imagining the fun we'll have worshiping in the language and manner of many different nations. I'm sure God will be smiling as all His people join in unity to worship Him. If only there were more unity now.

I believe it was the unity of heart, mind and message that caused God's presence to fill the Temple that day. God is always with us, however, there are times when He brings a greater weight of Himself. The truth is we humans can't contain God in His fullness.

Yes, He lives within us, but His fullness cannot be housed within our bodies. That's part of why He chose the Church as a corporate body in which He could live and through which he might express Himself.

There is so much more I could say about the importance of unity or oneness in Christ's body, the Bride. We must show love for one another. But for now, I will ask you to consider how you might become more one with your brothers and sisters in Christ so that we all may experience a greater presence of Him.

Can you even imagine how beautiful that would be! If all we want is His presence, I believe He will be pleased, and we will experience the revelation of Him in increasing measure. We must not desire Him only for what He does, but for the beauty of Who He is!

Day 203

What to Do when Words Hurt

2 Chronicles 6:12-8:10 / Romans 7:14-8:8
Psalm 18:1-15 / Proverbs 19:24-25

The strongest of people are sometimes tired. Warriors need rest just like anyone else. Then again, if we're in Christ, we're all warriors at one time or another. If you find yourself in a battle, remember that you have been equipped with your own personal armor. We have been given the belt of truth, the breastplate of righteousness, the shoes of the Gospel of peace, the shield of faith, the helmet of salvation and the sword of the Spirit. (See Ephesians 6:14-17).

Remember your armor, remember to pray, remember to keep your eyes on Jesus Christ the Commander of the Host of Heaven, and remember you are not wrestling against people, but against evil forces. It is the Lord who enables us to stand. It is the Lord who rescues and protects us.

In times when I feel someone is trying to whip my butt, I love reading passages like Psalm 18:1-3.

"I love you, LORD; you are my strength. The LORD is my rock, my fortress, and my savior; my God is my rock, in whom I find protection. He is my shield, the power that saves me, and my place of safety. I called on the LORD, who is worthy of praise, and he saved me from my enemies."

There you have it. When you feel you're up against something bigger than you, remember the Lord is your strength and place of safety. If there's a storm around you, hide in Him. If the words of others are assaulting you, put Him on as a shield. It would be nice to think we'll never have trouble, but it's not reality.

John 16:33 tells us, "I have told you these things, so that in me you may have peace. In this world you will have trouble. But take heart! I have overcome the world!"

We must know where to hide and how to fight. Our hiding place is Him and our greatest weapon is love. Remember what 1 Corinthians 13:13 tells us in The Passion Translation, "Above all else, let love be the beautiful prize for which you run."

If I'm running for love, all fear is gone. If I'm running for love, I cannot be or stay offended. That means I must immediately forgive in each situation that arises. If we're running for love, I win, you win, and we all win!

Day 204

How Do I Make the Right Choice?

2 Chronicles 8:11-10:19 / Romans 8:9-25
Psalm 18:16-36 / Proverbs 19:26

Choices. We have choices. Sometimes we think we don't. We believe we're a product of our upbringing, or that we are subject to the responses we give because of what's been done to us. You know the old saying, "the devil made me do it!". Yea, that's not true.

Sure, we respond the way we do based on the experiences we've had and the thoughts in our minds. We respond based on past hurts, betrayal, and suffering. However, when we look through the lenses of past pain, we are not able to see properly or clearly. And that's where the trouble begins.

Sometimes we're aware of the way we respond and sometimes we're not. Sometimes another person can try to help by talking to us about the problem. Sometimes we listen, and sometimes we are not able to hear them properly. No matter where we find ourselves in this scenario, there is freedom available. How do I know that?

Romans 8:9 says, "But you are not controlled by your sinful nature. You are controlled by the Spirit if you have the Spirit of God living in you."

Romans 8:12 says, "Therefore, dear brothers and sisters, you have no obligation to do what your sinful nature urges you to do."

I encourage you to read all of Romans 8:9-17 because it's so helpful to someone struggling to make the right choices. If we are in Christ, we have power over sin. That means we have the power within us to choose what is right and leave behind what is evil. But, of course, we still blow it from time to time! That's normal human behavior.

The power to do what's right doesn't come "from within us" in the sense that we can't muster up a right choice by the power of our will. The only power that will allow us to choose righteousness is the power of Holy Spirit. We can't be "good enough". We can't try to "be on our best behavior." None of that works.

We can't hold ourselves to this perfect standard, neither can we allow others to attempt to hold us to a standard of perfection. To allow that would be a spirit of religion and control, and that would grieve the Holy Spirit.

So, why do we attempt to hold ourselves and others to impossible standards of perfection? Is it so we can feel better about ourselves? Or to somehow feel we have measured up and are now acceptable to God and others? That doesn't work either.

Our only perfection is found through Jesus Christ. Our only hope of "being good" is because of God's Spirit in us. Everything that we have was given to us by Him. There is nothing we've earned or gained apart from His grace and goodness toward us. Once we realize this, there is nothing but thanksgiving in our hearts toward the One who has gifted us with all things.

Day 205

I Have Called You by Name

2 Chronicles 11-13 / Romans 8:26-39
Psalm 18:37-50 / Proverbs 19:27-29

All of us wonder why we were put here on earth, or what our purpose is. Are we simply marking time, or is there a reason we were born into this world during this exact moment in history? These are great questions that every person has likely asked. But to whom are we asking this question? And who has the answer?

Created beings must look to the One who is the Creator to find out their purpose and function. The beautiful things in creation also serve specific purposes. Our Creator knows the unique and beautiful purpose for each plant, animal, rock and body of water, and He values each of these created things.

If God created us in His image, and I believe He did, He is the One who knows our purpose. Let's read and study through a couple of verses from today's scriptures to help answer some of the questions regarding our purpose and our value to God.

Romans 8:29-30 reads, "For God knew His people in advance, and He chose them to become like His Son, so that His Son would be the firstborn among many brothers and sisters. And having chosen them, He called them to come to Him. And having called them, He gave them right standing with Himself. And having given them right standing, He gave them His glory."

What were God's actions in these two verses?

He knew – He chose – He called – He gave – He gave.

What does all that mean for us?

First, who doesn't relish the idea of being chosen? Do you remember in school when it was time for P.E. and the captains had to choose teams? No one wanted to be chosen last. Everyone wants to be chosen first but being chosen second or third is better than being chosen last. And being chosen is better than being left behind!

We feel loved knowing God chose us. Before He chose us, He knew us. How can that be?

In Psalm 139:16 we read:

"You saw who You created me to be before I became me! Before I'd ever seen the light of day, the number of days You planned for me were already recorded in Your book."

Even before we were created by our parents' union, God knew who we were. I think that's why my dad could name me three years before I was born! That knowledge was already out there in the Spirit world and my dad being a hearer of God's voice (even before He knew he belonged to God) heard God speak about his first child. God knew.

We are known and we are chosen. What else has God done for us? He invited us to come near Him. The verses in Romans say He "called" us which means "to utter in a loud voice, or to give a name to."

This is not just our given names that are being spoken of here. When God gives us a name, He is saying, "You are Mine." For those who are fans of The Chosen series, you will remember in season 1, episode 1 that Mary memorized the following verse as a child.

Isaiah 43:1, "But now, this is what the Lord says, He who is your Creator, Jacob, and He who formed you, Israel. 'Do not fear, for I have redeemed you, I have called you by name, you are Mine!'"

The Hebrew meaning for the word "name" is "a mark or memorial of individuality; by implication honor, authority, character." In other words, God is acknowledging that we are unlike anyone else and that He knows us intimately.

What about the final two statements? He gave us right standing, and He gave us His glory. He gave us right standing through Jesus Christ which means we have been made righteous or right with God in relationship. We are welcome to speak with Him any time.

What did He give us when He gave us His glory? The definition of glory is "to cause the dignity and worth of some person or thing to become manifest and acknowledged." My perspective on that is that God gave us His reputation, putting His stamp of approval on us because of Jesus Christ.

I hope you feel loved and encouraged by this short study! I sure do. I am in awe, as always, that the God of the universe would love us so much as to foreknow, choose, call, and give us the gifts of righteousness and His glory. I'm not sure we will grasp the weight of these gifts until we see Him face to face.

Day 206

Don't Forget to Say Your Prayers

2 Chronicles 14-16 / Romans 9:1-24 / Psalm 19 / Proverbs 20:1

I've been saying my prayers since I was a little girl, probably before I have a memory of it. My momma was saved in her teens, though she didn't really start a Christian path until later in life. My daddy was saved when I was maybe 4 or 5, so that's why I say I'm not sure when the prayers started.

Prayers are something that can seem intangible. We are talking to a God we can't see. There are times we may feel we're talking to ourselves, although we know by faith there is a loving Creator who is listening on the other side.

"Now I lay me down to sleep. I pray the Lord my soul to keep. If I should die before I wake, I pray the Lord my soul to take." Who remembers that prayer?

Lately, I've been pondering prayer and conversations with God. We are so used to popping into a time of prayer with a list of our needs, fears, wants and desires. But how often do we ask God how He is or what's on His heart? If we asked Him, our questions would likely be answered; if not directly, then indirectly.

As the Psalmist talked with God in chapter 19, he made a few requests of God in verses 12-13.

"How can I know all the sins lurking in my heart? Cleanse me from these hidden faults. Keep your servant from deliberate sins! Don't let them control me. Then I will be free of guilt and innocent of great sin."

There are times I'm painfully aware of my sins against God, and against the people I love. I also have sins that I hide within my heart such as unforgiveness, bitterness, and anger. There are times I've told myself that I just want to be angry for a bit and then I'll move on. But do I move on? And what does it mean to move on? If we don't resolve the contrary feelings in our hearts, we may accidentally allow an area of sin to form.

Maybe that's what David was concerned about when he asked God to cleanse him from hidden faults. And what about those deliberate sins? Those are the ones we know better than to engage in. We know what we're doing is grieving to Holy Spirit, but we assume because the sin is known only by us, we can get away with it. That is not true.

If we allow sin to remain, it gets bigger, deeper, and more involved over time. When our kids were little, we used to watch Veggie Tales. There is one episode titled Larry-Boy and the Fib from Outer Space! In this episode Junior Asparagus lies to his dad about an item that he broke in his house, blaming it on a sibling.

As Junior continues to tell lie after lie to cover up the original lie, the Fib gets larger and larger until it's a booming and scary figure that is terrifying to Junior. What's interesting is that Junior is immediately aware, just after the initial lie, that the Fib has grown, but he ignores the warning in his heart and continues along the path of deceit.

Finally, Junior realizes the situation has gotten out of control and he confesses to the lie and the cover-up of the lie. When he does, the Fib reduces little by little until it's back to its original size.

It takes a lot of courage and tenacity to admit to our faults and sin, but as we do God can bring healing and restoration into our lives. The pain of sin is then able to give way to the relief of the freedom that follows.

Scripture tells us in James 5:16 New Revised Standard Version, "Therefore confess your sins to one another, and pray for one another, so that you may be healed. The prayer of the righteous is powerful and effective."

It's humbling to admit our sins to one another, but when we do, relief pours into our hearts. All of us face these same temptations to sin. No one is above sin and temptation, so if we are willing to love one another enough to stand together in these times of confession, the whole community around us will be strengthened.

Say your prayers, be humble, and wait for God to heal your soul and cleanse your conscience. I promise the pain of confession and repentance are all worth it!

Day 207

Made Right with God

2 Chronicles 17-18 / Romans 9:25-10:13 / Psalm 20 / Proverbs 20:2-3

Salvation, being born again, giving our hearts to Jesus Christ, walking the aisle, going to the altar, and any other term one might use to indicate coming into right relationship with God is foundational to the Christian faith. One cannot call themselves a Christ follower apart from being made right with God through Jesus Christ.

Jesus Himself said,

"I am the Way, the Truth and the Life. No man comes to the Father, except through Me."— John 14:6.

Jesus is the only doorway or path to having a right relationship with God. I understand that many have tried other paths, but ultimately, before one passes from this life to the next, he or she must come face to face with the life of Jesus Christ and His sacrifice on the cross.

If it sounds like I'm preaching, I guess I am! What has made me so fired up? One of the portions of scripture from "The Romans Road" has me walking down memory lane. For those who aren't aware, "The Romans Road" refers to a body of scripture through the book of Romans which lays out the Gospel of salvation.

Romans 10:9-13 reads, "If you openly declare that Jesus is Lord and believe in your heart that God raised Him from the dead, you will be saved. For it is by believing in your heart that you are made right with God, and it is by openly declaring your faith that you are saved. As the Scriptures tell us, 'Anyone who trusts in Him will never be disgraced.' Jew and Gentile are the same in this respect. They have the same Lord, who gives generously to all who call on him. For 'everyone who calls on the name of the Lord will be saved.'"

God did not make it difficult for our relationship with Him to be restored. The relationship Adam and Eve had in the Garden of Eden with God is what God is restoring to us through Jesus Christ. For now, sin still interrupts our beautiful fellowship, but one day there will be a new Heaven and a new earth, and we will have unbroken connection with the One Who created and loves us.

While I am thankful for and appreciate the relationship I have with God today, I'm looking forward to seeing Him face to face. I'm looking forward to knowing Him the way He knows me. I'm looking forward to all the experiences of Heaven, the angels, the other saints who have gone before me, and the adventures I'll have jumping galaxies. Yes, that is what I plan to do after meeting Jesus!

Jeff and I have an ongoing funny conversation. I'm pretty sure our mansions will be side-by-side. He has such a love of food and people that I imagine him sitting on the front porch in his rocking chair, waiting for visitors to come share a meal with him.

And while I do love food and people, the adventurer in me can't wait to explore everything! I'm going to the throne room, the Heavenly temple, the crystal sea, the planets, and the galaxies. I want to travel! I want to explore. And when I've traveled and explored, I'll come back to sit on the porch with Jeff and share what I saw.

While we don't know what Heaven will be like, I do know we will never be bored. Worship, fellowship, food, and exploration are going to be amazing! And all of that is our inheritance because we said, "Yes" to the sacrifice Jesus made on our behalf.

I understand that some will say, "No" to the gift of our sin being wiped away on the cross – which was then sealed by Jesus's resurrection from the dead. That makes me unbearably sad. I can't imagine spending eternity apart from God with His love and light.

So, if you have not before, please consider these verses from Romans. Consider that they might just be the truth you can't live without. Pray and ask God to reveal Himself to you. If you say, "Yes" to Jesus Christ, I look forward to seeing you on one of my adventures in Heaven!

Day 208

Remember, The Battle is The Lord's

2 Chronicles 19-20 / Romans 10:14-11:12 / Psalm 21 / Proverbs 20:4-6

Sometimes, we feel like we are fighting battles we just can't win. A lot of times, we don't understand how we got into a battle-filled situation. Something has gone wrong, but we don't know what. We may be angry, confused, or sad. We may try to fix the problem ourselves only to end up making things worse. That's why we must learn to ask God for help in every situation.

In today's reading, the tribe of Judah along with King Jehoshaphat find themselves being attacked by three nations – the Moabites, the Ammonites and some of the Meunites. The first thing Jehoshaphat did was inquire of the LORD, proclaiming a fast among the people of Judah. Then Jehoshaphat prayed to God in front of all Judah. The verses below tell a small portion of the story.

2 Chronicles 20:12b reads, "We do not know what to do, but our eyes are on you." Then the Lord responded in verse 15 through Jahaiel, a descendant of the Levites and said, "Do not be afraid or discouraged because of this vast army. For the battle is not yours, but God's."

When the king didn't know what to do, he knew that he should keep his eyes on God. And we must do the same when we're unsure of what to do. No matter how we got into the situation, God has a solution. Not only does God have a solution, but He also knows what our response should be. Do we pray, fight, or stand still and allow God to fight on our behalf?

There are many other options the Lord may direct us toward, so listening is important. Sometimes we'll hear an answer right away, and sometimes we will need to patiently wait for God's response. Waiting for His response will give us the best possible outcome for the problem we're facing, so be sure not to jump ahead before hearing His voice.

The Lord answered the prayers and worked it out so that Jehoshaphat and his army didn't even have to fight. Jehoshaphat appointed men to sing to the LORD and to praise him for the splendor of His holiness. The singers went out at the head of the army, singing, "Give thanks to the LORD, for his love endures forever." (2 Chronicles 20:21).

As these men sang, the LORD set ambushes against the men of Ammon, Moab and Mount Seir who were invading Judah, and they were defeated. (2 Chronicles 20:22). By the time the armies of Judah arrived at the battlefield, the enemy armies had killed one another and all that was left to do was collect the plunder. Amazing!

Although the following verse from Psalm 21 refers to a different set of circumstances from King David's day, I found the words appropriate for how Jehoshaphat probably felt after the Lord delivered the tribe of Judah from her enemies.

Psalm 21:1 reads, "The king rejoices in your strength, LORD. How great is his joy in the victories you give!" Verse 7 says, "For the king trusts in the LORD; through the unfailing love of the Most High he will not be shaken."

Lord, we rejoice in Your strength! We are grateful that you have delivered us from all our enemies. We are grateful that we can come to You and You will provide answers for every situation we face. We give thanks to the Lord for His love endures forever!

Day 209

Does God Care about His Creation?

2 Chronicles 21-23 / Romans 11:13-36 / Psalm 22:1-18 / Proverbs 20:7

Have you ever looked around you and wondered where everything you see came from? I'm not talking about the trees you planted, the houses you built, or the cars you drive. Those were created or planted by men. What I'm asking is, "How did it all begin? Was there a "big bang", or an explosion, and suddenly everything was created and came into order?"

Logically I don't see how an explosion would have created order. Usually, an explosion creates destruction and chaos. If you love science, you've likely noticed patterns in the world around you. Flowers have petals that sprout from the center, and roses have concentric petals in layers. When snowflakes are placed under a microscope, they have beautiful, intricate patterns.

I could go on and on with examples from nature that prove a type of order and structure to life. Even our bodies have order and structure. For example, has anyone ever seen the helix and structure of our DNA or our cells under a microscope? It's fascinating.

I believe, as Genesis 1:1 explains,

"In the beginning God created the Heavens and the earth." John 1:1-3 tells us that, "In the beginning the Word already existed. The Word was with God, and the Word was God. He existed in the beginning with God. God created everything through him, and nothing was created except through Him."

I'm considering all these thoughts again because of what I read today in Romans 11:36.

"For everything comes from him and exists by His power and is intended for His glory. All glory to Him forever! Amen."

I believe the Bible when it says God created everything and that all things still have existence because of His power. Some believe God created everything, then left us to fend for ourselves. That belief is called Deism, which purports that God is unconcerned with and detached from His creation.

The verse in Romans tells us otherwise. Hebrews 1:3 confirms this; "...He sustains everything by the mighty power of His command..." This doesn't sound like an uninterested, distant God to me. I believe he is intimately involved and concerned with His creation.

There is another verse that proves God's loving concern for us. John 3:16 reads, "For this is how God loved the world. He gave his one and only Son, so that everyone who believes in Him will not perish but have eternal life."

He created all things. He keeps everything in order. He is lovingly concerned about everything. This describes only a small part of God's nature. God is love, so He will not leave His creation to implode and destroy itself, even though man certainly tries to destroy the earth's beauty!

It's important that we know God for Who He is and not according to the false ideas others may tell us. You will find the truth of His nature as you study scripture for yourself. That is part of why I wanted to read through the Bible again this year, and why I wanted to take you on this journey with me.

We cannot know God based only on what others tell us. We must see and hear the truth for ourselves. I encourage you to continue reading, studying, and asking questions. Don't believe something just because someone told you it's true. Read, listen, then ask God to reveal the truth. He will do it!

Day 210

We Are Running a Marathon

2 Chronicles 24-25 / Romans 12 / Psalm 22:19-31 / Proverbs 20:8-10

It's interesting to watch the different personality types and how they interact with others, but also to learn what they believe about themselves. I've met insecure people and confident people. I've also met people who cover their insecurity with confidence, and those who operate with false humility.

I define false humility as behaving as if you are incapable when you are fully capable and gifted in a certain area. False humility is a cover for insecurity, and not seeing yourself the way God does.

God is fully aware of who we really are. Most of us have a hard time understanding our God-design, and we also tend to be overly critical and harsh toward ourselves. So, how are we to get a proper estimation of who we really are and of what we are capable?

Romans 12:3 says this, "Because of the privilege and authority God has given me, I give each of you this warning: Don't think you are better than you really are. Be honest in your evaluation of yourselves, measuring yourselves by the faith God has given us."

How do we measure ourselves by the faith God has given us? Let's think of this faith as a pair of glasses that give us clear vision. We must know what our gifts, calling and purpose are in God's Kingdom. Once we're sure of these, we can operate as we know He has called and gifted us.

To operate in faith is to give neither more nor less weight to our place in the body. It is also to keep our eyes locked on the Father for His approval and not to be concerned with the approval of men.

We are perfect, righteous, forgiven, and clean because of Jesus. In Him we find our true destiny, purpose and calling. In Him we know that we are loved. We must look at ourselves through the lens of love because He is certainly looking at us in that way.

We know we have the Father's approval because He sees us through the blood of His much-loved Son. If we know our calling, and are walking securely in it, we can rest assured that we are pleasing God. But even more foundational to this point is that we are pleasing to God because we are His daughter or son. He is pleased simply in our existence as His.

You've heard the statement "stay in your lane." This statement applies to the way we operate within the body. If we "stay in our lane", we make space both for our gifts and the gifts of others. When we are secure enough to do this, we find ourselves growing in faith and becoming more content with our place in life.

I want to offer you an action plan. Pray, asking God to show you your part in His body. Once you hear His answer, begin to operate in that place according to your experience and knowledge, being careful not to run ahead. If you operate in your gifts, while also continuing to learn, you'll grow and become mature.

As I reminded a new friend recently, we are not sprinters; we are marathon runners. This means we don't have to quickly meet our finish line. Instead, we will pace ourselves, so we have strength to serve Him faithfully for many years. Let me leave you with one final verse for encouragement as we run the marathon.

Hebrews 12:1-2 English Standard Version says, "Therefore, since we are surrounded by so great a cloud of witnesses, let us also lay aside every weight, and sin which clings so closely, and let us run with endurance the race that is set before us, looking to Jesus, the founder and perfecter of our faith, who for the joy that was set before Him endured the cross, despising the shame, and is seated at the right hand of the throne of God."

To run with endurance is to run as a marathon or long-distance runner. We're in this race for the long-haul. Stay steady, stay in your lane, operate in your gift according to your faith and skill, and you will finish right on time!

Day 211

Responding to Those Who Govern

2 Chronicles 26-28 / Romans 13 / Psalm 23 / Proverbs 20:11

No doubt there are some crazy things happening in the elected (and unelected) governments around the world. There is corruption, self-serving motives, and blatant evil, along with a few righteous people of faith. So, how should Christians respond when governments in our nations have gone rogue? Romans 13:1-7 has me thinking about how we should live and respond to those in civil authority.

Romans 13:1-7 says, "Everyone must submit to governing authorities. For all authority comes from God, and those in positions of authority have been placed there by God. So, anyone who rebels against authority is rebelling against what God has instituted, and they will be punished. For the authorities do not strike fear in people who are doing right, but in those who are doing wrong. Would you like to live without fear of the authorities? Do what is right, and they will honor you."

Some may have a hard time with the language of being told to submit to civil authority. Some may also find it hard to believe God would put people into authority who do not have his heart. I have been in spaces where these verses were used to teach about authority in the church, even though that is not what's being taught here. I feel it's important for us to view this topic with the proper perspective.

Our first authority is God; as followers of Jesus, we submit ourselves to Him above all others. There are two thoughts that go along with that. If He is asking us to submit to authorities, even evil ones, we may do so and consider ourselves as submitting to Him in that. Second, there are reasons that civil authorities are put into place by God. Let's look at some of those reasons.

God desires to bless us, and that can be done when good men and women are in offices of government. God sometimes must judge a person, a people or a nation, and evil public servants are part of that judgment. When we sense we are either under judgment or that God's judgment is coming, we must remember that He wants to show mercy. Because of that, we must fast and pray for repentance and realignment of the people to God's ways.

Good public servants are put in place for our protection from evil. I understand that there are times when the public servants themselves are evil. However, it is important for us to want to honor both God and those in authority, remembering God intends for them to protect those of us who are doing what's right. The authorities should be responsible to punish those who are doing evil as a way of curbing evil.

Without structure and civil leadership, society would descend into chaos. Why? Because without Jesus Christ, men and women are evil in their hearts. It's hard to believe, but just as those of us who follow Jesus want to do what's right, those who follow the dark kingdom love to do evil. Evil doers are just as passionate about their worldview as we are about ours.

To review. Pray for those in leadership around you, asking God to bless them with His heart and vision. Ask Him how He wants you to serve your city, state, and nation beyond prayer. He may have more for you to do, so be willing to do your part in the realm of God's protection and justice in the earth.

If He asks you to run for office, do it. If He asks you to stay home and pray, do it. If He asks you to partner with other brothers and sisters in your region to declare His kingdom, do it. When it comes time to vote in regional and national elections, pray, do your research and vote. Do not remain silent.

"I urge you, first of all, to pray for all people. Ask God to help them; intercede on their behalf and give thanks for them. Pray this way for kings and all who are in authority so that we can live peaceful and quiet lives marked by godliness and dignity."—1 Timothy 2:1-2

Day 212

The Danger of Criticism

2 Chronicles 29 / Romans 14 / Psalm 24 / Proverbs 20:12

The title of this post is taken directly from Romans 14. The whole chapter is so good! There is unfortunately a lot of disagreement, arguing, even fighting within the body of Christ over things that do not matter. There are essential doctrines and there are non-essential doctrines. Faith in Jesus Christ for salvation is essential to our Christian faith. What we eat, or on which day we worship is not.

Maybe I'm stirring up a hornet's nest, but if one takes time to thoughtfully read this chapter, we'll see exactly what I'm speaking about. Then we won't be accountable to human words or opinions but to the words Holy Spirit wrote through the men He inspired.

The matter of who eats what has caused so much disagreement when it should cause none. Some believe eating meat is a sin, and some do not. Some believe drinking wine is a sin, and some do not. Some believe we should gather for fellowship on Saturdays, some on Sundays, and some believe the day doesn't matter at all if we love God and one another.

So, why do we argue over these things that don't matter? I believe, in part, that we argue because we love being right. Being right somehow affirms us as people; we feel validated. But Christianity is not about validation or about being right. Christianity is about serving others.

I will say that if you're searching for validation, that is found in an intimate relationship with Jesus Christ. If we are secure in our relationship with Him, we will understand His will for us. We'll know we are loved, and we will feel no need to look down on others for where they are in their journey.

And that's what this is about. When we criticize others for their choices, we are not allowing them and God to be in peaceful process together, and that shows a lack of love and understanding on our part. If we love the other person, we will receive them as they are. No matter someone's beliefs, let's leave the situation between them and God and continue to love them.

If your brother or sister is claiming to want to follow Jesus, and they are unaware of an area of sin, then while in the process of forming relationship with them the Lord may lead you to speak with them. Until He does, pray for them. And more than anything, love them. Love has an amazing way of giving space to others, allowing them to follow their desire for growth.

When we are loved, we want to change to please the one who loves us. As your family member or friend learns more about Jesus, they will begin to pattern their lives after Him, just like you are doing. We are much better friends if we allow others to follow Christ as we follow Him.

Life is simpler when we "mind our own hearts" and stop trying to mind someone else's heart. That never works out well for two reasons. One, we don't know their hearts, and two, God is the only one who fully understands what is in someone's heart. Not only that, but He has the solution and the path to lead them toward freedom in Him.

Let's be freedom givers by not placing stumbling blocks of unloving behavior in front of others. Let's love them as they are, trusting Holy Spirit to bring conviction when and where it's needed. He did that for us, and He will do that for them.

Day 213

Accept One Another

2 Chronicles 30-31 / Romans 15:1-22
Psalm 25:1-15 / Proverbs 20:13-15

Growing up, we were taught to be kind to everyone. Race, religion, social status – none of that mattered. People are people and are loved by God who created them in His image. Sure, there are people we get along with better than others. There are people whose personality rubs us the wrong way. That means not everyone will be in our "best friend" circle. That does not mean we are permitted to look down on anyone.

Scripture is filled with words that encourage us to love others and accept them as they are. There are two verses in Romans 15 that remind us how to treat others. Verse 5 says, "May God, who gives this patience and encouragement, help you live in complete harmony with each other, as is fitting for followers of Christ Jesus." Verse 7 says, "Therefore, accept each other just as Christ has accepted you so that God will be given glory."

"Live in complete harmony with each other." "Accept each other as Christ has accepted you." We have so many discussions in our home church about loving people as they are and not thinking too highly of ourselves. We had yet another discussion that wound around to this topic recently.

Why would we not accept another? I have two thoughts. The first is, for me to refuse to accept someone else is to believe I am somehow better than they are. Second, if my discernment tells me someone is dangerous, I do have the right to keep a watchful distance for my own safety.

But for the most part, people are kind and good and would not be harmful to me. The strong point I take away from these two verses is that Jesus Christ has accepted me in my sin and imperfection, now I am expected to accept others.

The word "accept" means "to take or receive into one's home, with the collateral idea of kindness, or to receive, i.e. grant one access to one's heart to take into friendship."

This is kind of a big deal. According to this definition, I am not just casually spending a little time with you; I am committing my life to yours. I also believe there must be an assumption that you are willing to do the same. I am not willing for this to be a one-sided acceptance. If I'm putting "skin in the game", I am expecting you to do the same.

I believe God is serious about our human relationships. As one who finds it difficult to trust people immediately, this is intimidating. And I will fully admit I'm not ready to do this with everyone. It takes me years to build a friendship to the point of trusting someone with intimate details of my life. There are only a few who fit this description.

I think it's good that not everyone is given access to the intimate details of one's life. I believe that in part because no one person has the capacity to hold space for more than a few people to this degree and level. I have many acquaintances, several friends, and a few intimate friends (my husband being at the top of that list).

I am, however, willing to love people as they are, without judgment or criticism. I need space to be and grow, as do you. If you find yourself in a community who loves you as you are and is willing to allow you to grow in Christ at His pace, you've found an immense gift. KEEP THOSE PEOPLE!

Day 214

Going Scorched Earth on Satan

2 Chronicles 32:1-33:13 / Romans 15:23-16:9
Psalm 25:16-22 / Proverbs 20:16-18

Thankfully, most of us do not have to engage in actual, physical battles as are fought in a war. Yes, we are engaged in a spiritual war that assaults our souls, but unless we have enlisted in the military, we will probably not have to use weapons such as guns against another human. However, some military strategies are still useful for those of us who fight spiritual battles.

Our highlighted verses for today are 2 Chronicles 32:1-4:

"After Hezekiah had faithfully carried out this work, King Sennacherib of Assyria invaded Judah. He laid siege to the fortified towns, giving orders for his army to break through their walls. When Hezekiah realized that Sennacherib also intended to attack Jerusalem, he consulted with his officials and military advisers, and they decided to stop the flow of the springs outside the city. They organized a huge work crew to stop the flow of the springs, cutting off the brook that ran through the fields. For they said, 'Why should the kings of Assyria come here and find plenty of water?'"

There is a military term called "Scorched Earth Policy," the meaning of which is "a military strategy that aims to destroy anything that might be useful to the enemy. Any assets that could be used by the enemy may be targeted, which usually includes obvious weapons, transport vehicles, communication sites, and industrial resources.

However, anything useful to the advancing enemy may be targeted, including food stores and agricultural areas, water sources, and even the local people themselves, though the last has been banned under the 1977 Geneva Convention."

King Hezekiah was using a partial "scorched earth policy" on the Assyrians by removing the water source that flowed outside the city. It's interesting that this military strategy (though not called that in Bible times) has been used for thousands of years.

A few years ago, having never heard this term before, Holy Spirit spoke these words to me, asking me to look up the meaning. I've talked about this a little bit before but wanted to go into greater depth today. Holy Spirit was leading me through an intense time of forgiveness and emotional healing. He was helping me remove from my soul many hindrances, and anything that might cause bitterness to take root.

When He spoke these words, I knew it was to help me understand that the difficulty I was walking through was necessary and for my own good. He also saw my future and knew I would require this type of concentrated soul work to answer God's call, not only in the next season but for the rest of my days.

I'm thankful God started me on a journey of living with this policy in mind. As I clear my soul on a regular basis, I'm forbidding the enemy from grabbing hold of anything in my life and being allowed to cause destruction. That means "going scorched earth" on the devil is to our benefit! Keeping our souls as clear as possible through repentance and forgiveness has become as important as devotional time. As a matter of fact, I recommend we use this process as part of our devotional time.

Day 215

Go Tell It on The Mountain

2 Chronicles 33:14-34:33 / Romans 16:10-27 / Psalm 26 / Proverbs 20:19

Who doesn't love to hear good news! Have you ever had someone say to you, "Which do you want first, the good news, or the bad news?" I'm one who prefers the bad news first so I can end with the good. I'm also hoping the good news will somehow outweigh the bad. Bad news is never easy to receive. But some are not even able to receive good news because their hearts are not prepared to believe something good is available for them.

Have you ever heard the gospel referred to as the "Good News?" I heard that term many times as a child in the 1970's. I haven't heard it as much lately. As a matter of fact, I don't hear the word "gospel" that much these days either.

Romans 16:25 states, "Now all glory to God, who is able to make you strong, just as my Good News says. This message about Jesus Christ has revealed His plan for you Gentiles, a plan kept secret from the beginning of time."

Some translations refer to the good news as "the gospel," as mentioned above. Most would assume this is the message about Jesus Christ, but what is included in this good news message?

The Greek word for "gospel" is defined as "the glad tidings of the kingdom of God soon to be set up, and subsequently also of Jesus the Messiah, the founder of this kingdom. After the death of Christ, the term comprises also the preaching of (concerning) Jesus Christ as having suffered death on the cross to procure eternal salvation for the men in the kingdom of God, but as restored to life and exalted to the right hand of God in Heaven, thence to return in majesty to consummate the kingdom of God."

If someone tells you they are preaching the gospel, they are sharing the truth about Jesus Christ the Messiah who has already come. They are preaching the gospel of salvation. Not everyone believes Jesus, or the Messiah, has come, or that Jesus Christ was God in the flesh. However, when we share the truth from God's Word, we are sharing words that are backed by His Spirit, so they are "alive" and able to draw a person's heart toward the truth.

Hebrews 4:12 states, "For the word of God is alive and powerful. It is sharper than the sharpest two-edged sword, cutting between soul and spirit, between joint and marrow. It exposes our innermost thoughts and desires."

We don't have to try to convince anyone of the truth. The truth is powerful enough to convince all on its own just by us being willing to share. If someone is ready to hear, they will receive. If one is not ready to receive, the words will still go into their hearts and will be considered. Who knows what the fruit of your sharing may be.

The bottom line is there is no need to stress about trying to make someone believe your message. It is Holy Spirit's job to convince others, the Father's heart to draw them to Himself, and our job to speak. If you knew your only role was speaking, would that make it easier to share when you sense there is an opportunity?

We are not responsible for the outcome, only for the delivery. So, when it's on our heart to share, we may simply share, pray, and leave the results up to God. No one enjoys being hounded about any message, whether it's the gospel or a marketing campaign.

Day 216

Honor Your Parents

2 Chronicles 35-36 / 1 Corinthians 1:1-17
Psalm 27:1-6 / Proverbs 20:20-21

Sometimes children grow up and become friends with their parents, and sometimes they never see eye-to-eye. My parents were raised in a generation where kids were meant to remain in the role of children, and close friendships were not on the radar.

My mom was raised with a Quaker background where children were to be seen and not heard. Despite all these obstacles, my dad and I developed a bond of friendship, but with my mom it was a harder journey.

I have always seen my husband and children as some of my favorite people. Jeff is my best friend, and I really wanted our children to grow into friends. I believe our hard work together has created that as best we can. My adult children and I don't see the world the same in every area but then again, who does. I don't believe we must agree on everything to love and be kind to one another, even with our differing views.

At some point I began calling Jeff, Matthew, Katherine, Abigail, and I "the five family." In some ways, we are the beginning of the generations that will come after us, even though we are building on those who were here before us. In addition to our five, we have a son-in-law who we adore and four grandbabies who are our world. We are extremely blessed.

Even though my parents and I had a difficult time relating to one another, I was taught to respect and honor them. If you had horrible or abusive parents, that is certainly harder, and I'm sorry you suffered in that way. It's hard to respect someone who misuses you.

All that said, there are times we read something in scripture that seems harsh. Today, I read Proverbs 20:20 and thought I had better take a closer look. As I considered taking that closer look, I thought it wise to reflect on my own experiences with my parents.

The verse states,

> "If you insult your father or mother,
> your light will be snuffed out in total darkness."

That's blunt. Did you also notice there were no qualifications regarding whether they were good or bad parents? The word "insult" means "to make light of or to show contempt (hatred) toward."

What does that verse mean when it says, "your light will be snuffed out?" It sounds like one of those old movies when they said, "Lights out," and they meant they were going to put a hit out to kill someone. But that's not what this means.

When I looked up the word "light" in Hebrew the meaning referred to "a lamp, or that by which one sees." What I conclude from this is that if we choose to treat our parents with contempt, we will no longer be able to see the truth. We will be blinded, lost, confused, and wandering.

Since God does not treat us according to what our sins deserve (Psalm 103:10), shouldn't we offer the same love and kindness to others, especially to our family? Again, I understand that if your parents were abusive this is a hard verse to reconcile. But if you're in Christ, I encourage you to sit with the two truths before you and see what God might say.

As a reminder, forgiveness is for us, not necessarily for the other person. I believe this verse is the same. Truth is for the hearer, or the one being confronted with it. If you listen and follow the path of that truth, you will be the one who benefits. The other person will gain nothing until they are also face-to-face with the truth.

We have a choice. We can read this truth and walk away, or we can read this truth and ask God what truth is there for us. I'm reading and asking. What about you?

Day 217

Mind Your Own Business

Ezra 1-2 / 1 Corinthians 1:18-2:5 / Psalm 27:7-14 / Proverbs 20:22-23

It's difficult to know how to respond when someone continually persecutes you. It's even tougher to navigate and understand when it's someone who claims the name of Christ. Should we not treat one another with forgiveness and kindness, even when misunderstandings have occurred in the past? I believe that as followers of Christ, we should be the first to forgive, bless and move on.

When I read Psalm 27:11-12 I was reminded of an ongoing situation in my past where my family was being spoken of evilly. I tried to make sense of it. I forgave, prayed, fasted, and blessed them. Eventually, the Lord released us to continue to move forward regardless of what others were doing or saying behind the scenes.

> "Teach me Your way, LORD; lead me in a straight path
> because of my oppressors. Do not turn me over to the desire
> of my foes, for false witnesses rise up against me,
> spouting malicious accusations." —Psalm 27:11-12

David certainly faced many enemies, the chief of which was King Saul. King Saul was both demon-oppressed and jealous of David. Saul attempted to kill David on several occasions, causing David to have to hide in caves for months. David knew he had been anointed as king, but I think he understood it was not yet his time to reign. David also purposefully honored Saul because he was God's anointed king.

In this prayer to God, David is asking the Lord to help him understand the right perspective. David is aware that when facing an enemy, the path of human reasoning will not be effective. He knows he needs God's wisdom and insight to properly face this enemy while maintaining his integrity. We would be wise to wait to respond toward our enemies until we know God's heart in the situation.

When David was asking to be led in a straight path, he was asking God to give him "level ground upon which to walk, knowing difficulties are current and ongoing." The commentaries I read clarified this as part of David's request.

He was asking to be made aware of the traps of the enemy. And trust me, the enemy would love to trap us in anger, unforgiveness and bitterness when an enemy continues to attack us.

Next David offers a plea for safety and protection by in essence saying, "Please don't let my enemies catch me and get their way!" God has a way, a plan, and a purpose for us, and it is to bring forgiveness, healing and blessing into our lives, not the wished-for destruction from our enemies.

The enemy may try to trap us by causing us to wish evil upon our enemies. Don't do it! Forgive them, bless them, and pray for them. They obviously need God's love and perspective.

David knew he was being falsely accused, not because he was a perfect man who was without sin but because he was doing all he knew to do to honor God and his enemies in the situation.

I used to say I didn't have any enemies, except one, the devil. I'm sad to say now that I have those who behave as enemies. It shouldn't be this way in the body of Christ.

If Jesus followers can't get along with and forgive one another, there is no way the world will want what we have. When we behave this way, we end up looking just like the people who are lost without Jesus. Our behavior makes it appear as if we do not possess the eternal life Jesus died to give us. That is more than sad; it's an enemy plot to keep the lost from seeing the truth.

To the best of my ability, I refuse to be a tool of the devil. I do not comply. I'm reminded of another scripture from Romans 12:18, New American Standard Bible. "If possible, so far as it depends on you, be at peace with all people."

For my part, I will not engage in speaking evil of another brother or sister. I know it grieves the heart of the Father when we do this. However, I have no control over what others say and do. That is between them and God.

Mind your own business, work hard, love others and move on. Our final verse is 1 Thessalonians 4:11 which says, "Make it your goal to live a quiet life, minding your own business and working with your hands, just as we instructed you before."

Day 218

Taking Away the Rights of The Enemy

Ezra 3:1-4:23 / 1 Corinthians 2:6-3:4 / Psalm 28 / Proverbs 20:24-25

I love good mysteries! As a matter of fact, when I was young, I used to read two book series: One Minute Mysteries and Two Minute Mysteries. I adored those books! They made my brain work so hard and just like a lot of the Sherlock Holmes series, the clues always led to solving what had occurred. I still enjoy a good mystery movie, or any movie that "twists" your brain.

So, any time I've read in the Bible that God has mysteries, I've been fascinated to solve the clues and gain the revelation. The good news is, because we have God's Spirit, we can understand the mysteries spoken of in scripture.

1 Corinthians 2:6-7 says, "Yet when I am among mature believers, I do speak with words of wisdom, but not the kind of wisdom that belongs to this world or to the rulers of this world, who are soon forgotten. No, the wisdom we speak of is the mystery of God —his plan that was previously hidden, even though he made it for our ultimate glory before the world began."

The essence of God's mysteries contains His wisdom and plans for us. He does not want His mysteries hidden from those of us who are His. The word "mystery" means "generally mysteries, religious secrets, confided only to the initiated and not to ordinary mortals. Of God: the secret counsels which govern God in dealing with the righteous, which are hidden from ungodly and wicked men but plain to the godly."

In Christ Jesus, we have access to truth that those who are not in Christ do not have. Which is as it should be! For the enemy to know all the mysteries would mean that he could more easily gain an upper hand over us, and we need all the help we can get against his schemes! We need a few tricks up our sleeves and Jesus knows that.

Jesus was aware of the enemy's tricks, and He was determined not only to reconcile us to the Father but also to gain an advantage for us against the devil. Before we are in Christ, we are "devil fodder" – open to any and every attack and misuse of the enemy. But once we are in Christ, the mystery is that we are safe and hidden in Him, able to benefit from every resource He has.

We have become His heirs and everything He has is ours. This is another truth previously hidden from our enemy. I believe that's part of why satan hates us, because we have been given an inheritance as daughters and sons and there is nothing he can do to take that from us!

The ultimate trickery was Jesus's willing death on the cross. Jesus knew, though the devil did not, that His death would gain our freedom from sin. Jesus knew that when He went into hell, he would take back the authority that had been given to satan when Adam and Eve were attacked and tricked in the garden and ultimately disobeyed God. Another mystery is that we have the authority of Jesus Christ, and we have been given permission to operate fully in that authority as daughters and sons.

This means we can laugh "all the way to the bank!" We have already won the war through Jesus Christ. The devil wins absolutely nothing in the lives of those who are in Christ. That's why it's important for us to know who we are and what we've been given. The enemy will only be able to fool us when we are unaware of our rights. Once we know who we are and are fully aware of what that means, he no longer has any hold over us!

The Bible is not a one- or two-minute mystery type read; how-ever, I encourage you to read some every day so you will know your rights through Jesus Christ. Too many believers are walking around being robbed by the devil because they do not know what they have been given. I say, "No more!" Know your rights, operate in them, and help others do the same.

Day 219

All of Us Together

Ezra 4:24-6:22 / 1 Corinthians 3:5-23 / Psalm 29 / Proverbs 20:26-27

Humans live in houses, animals live in holes and dens, but where does God live? In the Old Testament the answer to that question varied. Yes, He lives in Heaven, but also God is everywhere.

When the people who descended from Israel (Jacob) left Egypt, God lived in a pillar of cloud by day and a pillar of fire by night. When the tabernacle was built in the desert, God lived above the ark, between the Cherubim. And again, when Solomon built the beautiful temple at Jerusalem, God lived above the ark, between the Cherubim.

1 Corinthians 3:16 states, "Don't you realize that all of you together are the temple of God and that the Spirit of God lives in you?"

I had not before noticed that all of us together create a temple. 1 Corinthians 6:19 says, "Don't you realize that your body is the temple of the Holy Spirit, who lives in you and was given to you by God?"

God "came upon" men and women in the Old Testament and up until Jesus Christ incarnated (became a man) on the earth. Once Jesus arrived, He was the first in Whom the Spirit of God resided. There was no opportunity for God's Spirit to live within us until after Jesus's crucifixion, burial, resurrection, and ascension.

Jesus told His disciples for months that He was going to be

leaving them and going back to His Father, but they had no frame of reference for such things. They didn't understand what Jesus meant.

Jesus told them in John 16:5-7,

"But now I am going away to the one who sent me, and not one of you is asking where I am going. Instead, you grieve because of what I've told you. But in fact, it is best for you that I go away, because if I don't, the Advocate won't come. If I do go away, then I will send him to you."

How could it be better that Jesus went away after He and the disciples had spent the past 3 years together forming friendships? They probably thought they would continue to live in community with one another for the rest of their lives.

We know from scripture that they also believed Jesus had come to set up an earthly kingdom to set them free from Roman oppression. That, however, was not Jesus's plan. They were so slow to understand, just as we sometimes are.

Jesus knew why He had come; to reconcile us in relationship to His Father. I say "reconcile" because when Adam and Eve were attacked in the Garden of Eden, we lost our intimate friendship with God. It was always the plan of the Father to provide a way for us to be in close communion with Him again.

The advantage of Jesus's leaving was that just as He had lived with Holy Spirit living within Him, He was going to send Holy Spirit to live within His followers. A new day was coming! The power that was around the disciples was now going to live in them.

Why is that an advantage? Because Jesus was one person while on earth, not able to be everywhere at once as God's Spirit is able to be. We also are only able to be in one place at a time as we carry God's

Spirit. However, if all of God's followers are filled with Holy Spirit, we can carry and release the Holy Spirit to anyone with whom we come in contact. Score!

So, our bodies are a temple, and we as Christ's body on earth are also a corporate temple. Talk about power on earth! Let's keep our personal temples, as well as the temple of Christ's body, free from sin, and let's treat these temples with the love and grace of Jesus.

Day 220

Our Stamp of Approval

Ezra 7:1-8:20 / 1 Corinthians 4 / Psalm 30 / Proverbs 20:28-30

I used to care what people thought about me. Honestly, I still care, but less than I used to. I'm working on that. If I am living my life for an audience of One, I should be concerned only with His thoughts toward me.

It is the Lord who sees my heart, my motives and my actions and will judge based on the full picture of the truth of my life. So, why do I allow the thoughts of others toward me to cause me pain or joy? Good question.

The whole chapter of 1 Corinthians 4 is thought-provoking, and I found many portions that were worthy of study, but I decided to dive into verse 5 because it spoke to so many of the seasons I've walked through. Along with working through caring what others think, I've been working through ridding myself of insecurity. It is only when we see ourselves through the eyes of the Father that we become fully secure and unashamed.

1 Corinthians 4:5 reads, "Therefore judge nothing before the appointed time; wait until the Lord comes. He will bring to light what is hidden in darkness and will expose the motives of the heart. At that time each will receive their praise from God."

First, we are to judge nothing. It is God's job to judge. Sometimes we are quick to judge someone, writing them off for whatever shortcomings we see. However, their story has not been fully written.

There is always time for one to change or become more like

Jesus, especially if they are hearing and obeying Him. The wrap up of our story doesn't come until the end of our lives, after we have walked through trials, persevered, grown and matured into who God has called us to be.

Some of us will accomplish a lot of what is on God's heart for us, some a moderate portion, and some a small taste of God's plans He prepared for us. But, again, it is not for our fellow humans to decide how much of that plan we accomplished or how well we performed. I'm thankful to have my merciful Jesus as my Judge. Wait until the Lord comes; He will judge.

When Jesus does judge, it will be about the motives of one's heart, not about the tasks accomplished. Many people do good things but for the wrong reason.

God wants to speak to us about why we did the things we did. Did we love and help others so they would like us? Or so we could appear to be mature or wise? Or did we love and help others because Jesus asked us to, regardless of what people thought?

It is our motives that are hidden in the dark places of our hearts. God will shine His loving light on our hearts so that we will understand what our motives were during different seasons of life. Hopefully we recognized why we were acting in certain ways and shifted toward the heart of the Father to guide us in the good things we accomplished.

At the end of the verse, it states that at the time of judgment each will receive her or his praise from God. This reminds me of another verse in Colossians 3:23 that reads, "Work willingly at whatever you do, as though you were working for the Lord rather than for people."

We must work for God and serve people. We are approved by God, and we love people. It's important to differentiate between these because if we do not, we will begin seeking the approval of men when it is only God Who can approve us. We serve people because they are loved by God, not so we can gain something from them.

Day 221

Judge Sin with a Heart of Love

Ezra 8:21-9:15 / 1 Corinthians 5 / Psalm 31:1-8 / Proverbs 21:1-2

I'm going to tackle a concept from scripture that has caused some controversy in the church over the years. At times we hear things spoken from scripture and many times the words are taken out of context or are misinterpreted making them difficult to understand and follow. If you are a Christian, you will want to know and follow the Word of God. To follow God's words, we must properly understand what is written.

In Matthew 7:1 it states,

> "Do not judge others, and you will not be judged.
> For you will be treated as you treat others.
> The standard you use in judging is the standard
> by which you will be judged."

You are probably already nervous for me, but we will walk through this topic together prayerfully, if not perfectly. Before we dive into this controversial topic, I want to quote two verses from today's reading.

1 Corinthians 5:12-13, "It isn't my responsibility to judge outsiders, but it certainly is your responsibility to judge those inside the church who are sinning. God will judge those on the outside; but as the Scriptures say, 'You must remove the evil person from among you.'"

Let's put this scripture into context. The "evil person" spoken of is a man who is within the community of believers in Jesus Christ, so he is claiming to be a Christian. However, he is actively involved in a sexual relationship with his father's wife.

The Enduring Word Commentary I read when I researched these verses points out that not only is this sin unacceptable within the church, but it is also heavily condemned even among the non-believers in the area. This man's sin is affecting himself, his father, his father's wife, the community of believers he is committed to, and the community of nonbelievers around them. This man is living a lifestyle of a nonbeliever. I say that because God's Word teaches specifically against sex outside of marriage.

If Jesus Christ is meant to live within us by faith, and we are meant to be on a journey of being conformed to His image, willful sin has no place within us. Once we are aware that our behavior is sinful, we must repent and make another choice. This man appears to be aware of, but unwilling to repent from, his sin.

By the believers around him ignoring his sin, they are not allowing him the freedom in Christ that Jesus died to give us. There is also the matter of the nonbelieving people outside the church recognizing that perhaps this life of devotion to Christ has no power or is no different than the lives they are currently living. If that is the case, why would anyone want to listen to the message of the Church?

When we judge others, we must first examine our own lives and make a judgment there. We must ask ourselves if we are engaging in the very thing we are judging within another. If so, we are behaving as hypocrites and must first take care of our own sin. If we are pure from the sin we are seeing in others, it is loving of us to address the sin, but only if Holy Spirit asks us to. But before we jump straight into judgment, we must follow a protocol.

I'll call this the Matthew 18 protocol.

Matthew 18:15-17 reads,

"If another believer sins against you, go privately and point out the offense. If the other person listens and confesses it, you have won that person back. But if you are unsuccessful, take one or two others with you and go back again, so that everything you say may be confirmed by two or three witnesses. If the person still refuses to listen, take your case to the church. Then if he or she won't accept the church's decision, treat that person as a pagan or a corrupt tax collector."

Judgment does not come into effect until after we have attempted to follow these steps. Speak privately to your beloved brother or sister about their sin. If they will not listen, take one or two more trusted, mature believers with you to speak to that one, remembering that this is a process of love and restoration and not of condemnation. Even if the brother or sister will not listen and must be removed from fellowship with you, you must maintain an attitude of love and prayer, believing that God will convict, bring repentance, then restore the one you love.

This is not about condemnation; this process is with the hope of restoring someone you love to right relationship with God and with the community of believers. If you have been treated in a way that fell outside these parameters and were hurt by them, may I tell you that I'm so sorry. Everything we do within the community of Jesus followers must be done in love and with the heart to restore. Otherwise, we are not operating with the heart of the Father.

I hope this entry brings clarity to this difficult topic. Above all else, when dealing with matters of sin, approach those you love with humility and a heart to restore them to spirit, soul and body health.

Day 222

Clean up on Aisle Ten

Ezra 10 / 1 Corinthians 6 / Psalm 31:9-18 / Proverbs 21:3

Pleading and bargaining... making excuses... avoiding the truth... all these are possible responses when we're "caught" doing something wrong. "I'll do better next time." "I didn't know it was wrong."

Have you ever personally felt terrible when you've done something you should not have? Even if no one tells us, we are innately aware when we are off track. Most of us were raised being taught right from wrong.

Romans 2:14-16 states, "Even Gentiles, who do not have God's written law, show that they know his law when they instinctively obey it, even without having heard it. They demonstrate that God's law is written in their hearts, for their own conscience and thoughts either accuse them or tell them they are doing right. And this is the message I proclaim—that the day is coming when God, through Christ Jesus, will judge everyone's secret life."

Each of us is born with that sense of right and wrong because of God's law being written on our hearts. This sense of right and wrong is separate from salvation or the new birth. Even those who reject Jesus Christ have a sense of moral right and wrong. I've met some of the most loving and kind people who do not follow Jesus Christ.

The verse from today's reading that has me considering these thoughts is Proverbs 21:3 which states:

"The Lord is more pleased when we do what is right and just than when we offer Him sacrifices."

This also reminds me of the exchange between Saul and Samuel after Saul offered the sacrifice without waiting for Samuel. Saul was told to wait to offer sacrifices until Samuel arrived, but when Samuel was delayed Saul offered the sacrifice without the prophet. Not only did Saul not obey the prophet, but it was also inappropriate according to God's law for Saul as the king to make such an offering.

The first thing Saul did was make excuses about why he didn't wait for Samuel. Doing what was right by waiting would have been simpler, although not easy for Saul since his men were growing restless and threatening to leave him instead of waiting for the expected battle with the Philistines. His impulsive behavior cost him the kingdom, and God's blessing was removed from him that day.

What about you and me? How often do we request something from God, then grow impatient in the waiting? Many times, there is nothing we can do to change the situation apart from waiting for God to work. However, there are instances when we could do something to alleviate our suffering. But if God has told us to wait, then we must wait. If God gives instructions to go ahead in an area, it is permissible to move ahead.

The statement regarding us offering Him sacrifices points to our excuse-making or to our response of trying to make it right by performing another action. If we blow it by not obeying God in an area, our very best response is to ask forgiveness in humility. God will forgive us. There may be a consequence that has been set into motion by our disobedience, but God's grace will meet us even in the consequence.

You've heard the statement that it's easier to get forgiveness than to ask permission. The only problem with that statement is the

baggage you'll end up carrying. Permission brings no baggage. Forgiveness usually demands a clean-up crew. I'd rather ask permission,
or better yet, know God's Word and follow it to the best of my ability
and understanding.

So, the next time you have a choice of obedience or your own
bright ideas, I advise obedience. It may irk your flesh but, in the end,
you'll be glad you made that choice. Your heart and mind will be clear
and there will be no need for a broom or mop.

Day 223

Becoming like Jesus

Nehemiah 1:1-3:14 / 1 Corinthians 7:1-24
Psalm 31:19-24 / Proverbs 21:4

So often we believe we must change to be accepted by God and people. What we are not always aware of is that God accepts us as we are, not just at our salvation but throughout the process of becoming more like Him.

Our lives are meant to be a process of becoming like Jesus. We will not reach a stage of perfection on earth. Complete perfection does not come until we are given a new body in eternity.

As we begin to change, it can be difficult for most of us to be content with who we are and with the process we are in. We can be hard on ourselves and not always willing to extend grace. But we must extend grace, especially to ourselves and of course, to others.

There are several verses in 1 Corinthians 7 that address a different side of our new life in Christ. As we are changing the way we think, act and respond, we may be considering the need to change other areas of our lives. We may find ourselves becoming discontented with outward circumstances. Let's address this part of our new life before talking more about the exciting inward changes that will be taking place.

1 Corinthians 7:20 states, "Yes, each of you should remain as you were when God called you."

The verses prior to this verse speak about circumcision, which points to Jewish versus Gentile beliefs during this time in history. The verses that follow verse 7 speak about slavery and freedom, because that was part of the culture at that time.

In that time, if one were a Jew (circumcised), he was free to remain that way. If one were a Gentile (uncircumcised), he was also free to remain that way. If one were a slave, he was free to remain so and if one was free, he was free to remain so. But what does all this mean for us?

Personal application in our society would tell us to keep our jobs, stay in our faith communities (unless they teach against scripture), stay within and connected to our families, and stay married to our spouse. Once we have experienced an inward change because of Jesus, we do not necessarily need to make a sudden outward change in our circumstances.

The changes we will make have more to do with our new way of thinking as mentioned above. As our choices change, our character will change. It is expected of a follower of Jesus to become more like Jesus Christ with each passing day, week, and year. If our behavior is not outwardly changing, we may be stuck and in need of some discipleship.

You've heard the statement that you can't put lipstick on a pig. A pig is still a pig, even with lipstick. A Christian is one inwardly first, and over time, his behavior begins to change.

The people around you will become aware that something is different. Your friends will see changes in you as you learn more about being like Jesus Christ. As you study His Word and connect with a Christian community, you will begin to think and act like the new person that you are.

It is by grace we are saved, and it is by grace we continue to be transformed into a person who more resembles the heart of the Father. Our goal must be to be like Jesus Christ. We will begin to model our lives after the life He showed us when He was on earth. To do that, we must recognize where we fall short, intentionally shift and change, and continue to align our hearts with scripture.

Day 224

Disciples Who Make Disciples

Nehemiah 3:15-5:13 / 1 Corinthians 7:25-40
Psalm 32 / Proverbs 21:5-7

As followers of Jesus Christ, we have priorities regarding where we spend our time and energy. Many get their priorities backward and it causes deficits in every area. However, when we have first things first, our lives are filled with both peace and productivity.

If we are not filled with God's Spirit, along with receiving the rest we require, we will not be able to help anyone else. Have you ever tried to work at your job or care for your family when you're exhausted? You end up making mistakes and sometimes taking up much more time having to re-do tasks because you are not at your best.

I promise there are enough hours in the day to care first for yourself, then your family, then others. Part of caring for yourself as a follower of Jesus is quiet time spent with Him. Build that relationship with Jesus first, then build your family, then your friend relationships. You will have time for everything when done in the proper order.

As I was reading Nehemiah, which is a book in the Bible that I really enjoy, I was interested by the fact that as each family worked to rebuild the walls of Jerusalem, many of them worked on the wall right across from their own home. I see this as these families wisely considering their own safety first so that they could later be responsible for the safety of others.

There is also the aspect that as each family took care of his own section of the wall, the community was made stronger. Because of the attacks of those who opposed the building of the wall, many worked with building materials in one hand and a weapon in the other. The community also took turns guarding and building. If they had not worked together, the wall would not have been rebuilt and all of them would have been open to attack.

By taking care of your own soul, you are also contributing to the strength of your family and community of friends. If you are part of a church community, they are thankful for your strength. You can quietly know that you are contributing to the success of all as you work to strengthen yourself in the Lord.

Perceiving life from this perspective certainly puts the traditional views of church life into question. You know the views; the ones that believe the man or woman behind the pulpit is responsible for all the feeding and all the tending. Those who do church life this way are burning themselves out while not allowing the body to be released into their gifts and callings. This is a disservice to all Christ's body.

The one who teaches and disciples you must feed you with the intent of you learning not only to feed yourself, but also that you will learn to feed others. To make disciples, we must keep this cycle going of teaching others to feed themselves. That does not mean we are teaching them to exist alone. We are simply teaching them to eat for themselves first, then to come into the community to learn and to help others.

Matthew 28:19-20 tells us,

"Now wherever you go, make disciples of all nations, baptizing them in the name of the Father, the Son, and the Holy Spirit. And teach them to faithfully follow all that I have commanded you. And never forget that I am with you every day, even to the completion of this age."

Jesus told his followers to make disciples. As His followers today, we must not only be His disciples, but we must also teach others to be His disciples. I believe you can teach someone even if you are only one step ahead of them in your learning, or even if you are learning together and you have a heart to show another what you're learning.

There are no special qualifications required other than you must be born again, filled with God's Spirit, and willing to help others in their growth. We need more people like that in the Church.

We need those who will feed themselves and help others do the same. Where do you see yourself in this picture? Self-evaluation is important, so take time today to ask God where you fit into this scenario for church growth.

Day 225

Choose Love above All

Nehemiah 5:14-7:73 / 1 Corinthians 8
Psalm 33:1-11 / Proverbs 21:8-10

Which is of more value, knowledge, power, or love? Knowledge is helpful because it can keep one out of trouble and help us get ahead in life. Power can keep us safe and give us influence. Love seems all "ooshie-gooshie" and soft, so how can love be of any benefit? What if I told you that love is true power? Let's begin with proof that love is powerful!

1 Corinthians 8:1b-2 tells us:

"But while knowledge makes us feel important, it is love that strengthens the church. Anyone who claims to know all the answers doesn't really know very much."

Romans 2:4 in The Passion Translation reads, "Do the riches of His extraordinary kindness make you take Him for granted and despise Him? Haven't you experienced how kind and understanding He has been to you? Don't mistake His tolerance for acceptance. Do you realize that all the wealth of His extravagant kindness is meant to melt your heart and lead you into repentance?"

John 3:16 in The Passion Translation reads, "For here is the way God loved the world – He gave His only, unique Son as a gift. So now everyone who believes in Him will never perish but experience everlasting life."

It is love that strengthens the church, melts our hearts, leads us to repentance, and causes us to receive eternal life.

Now let's look at knowledge to see what we might learn. Above, 1 Corinthians tells us that knowledge makes us feel important. I guess that means it feeds our ego, giving us a false sense of security and prominence. That could be of benefit here on earth, but what about in our eternity? What does knowledge gain for us?

Proverbs 1:7 says this about knowledge:

"The fear of the Lord is the beginning of knowledge;
fools despise wisdom and instruction."

The word for "knowledge" in 1 Corinthians means "indicative of intelligence or understanding. The word for "knowledge" in Proverbs 1:7 refers to "discernment, skill, and wisdom."

There are slight differences in the two words, aside from the fact that they are written in two different languages and may have different understandings in that regard alone. Intelligence or understanding speaks to our natural or human reasoning. Again, I'm not saying to attain human knowledge is wrong, but it appears to be of less benefit than the knowledge spoken of in Proverbs.

The word "knowledge" in Proverbs is speaking of spiritual wisdom or wisdom that comes not from our own human minds, but from God's Spirit. This type of knowledge is of more benefit than human knowledge. Yet both are less important than love. I want to offer one more portion of scripture for proof of the power of love.

I Corinthians 13:1, 13 in The Passion Translation reads, "If I were to speak with eloquence in earth's many languages, and in the Heavenly tongues of angels, yet I didn't express myself with love, my words would be reduced to the hollow sound of nothing more than a clanging cymbal. Until then, there are three things that remain: faith, hope, and love – yet love surpasses them all. So, above all else, let love be the beautiful prize for which you run."

Love surpasses them all – if you read the whole chapter, you'll notice all the good things that are mentioned such as knowledge, prophecies, riddles, and mysteries, and of course ending with faith and hope. Yet Holy Spirit tells us all through scripture that love surpasses all these things. It was because of love that the Father sent His Son Jesus to suffer and die on our behalf.

I believe love is the ultimate power that held Jesus on the cross. The fact that He died willingly in obedience to His Father and on our behalf speaks more love than any of us will ever know apart from God's perfect love. One final portion of scripture tells us how Jesus felt upon considering His impending death on the cross.

Philippians 2:7-8 in The Passion Translation reads, "Instead He emptied himself of His outward glory by reducing Himself to the form of a lowly servant. He became human! He humbled Himself and became vulnerable, choosing to be revealed as a man and was obedient. He was a perfect example, even in His death – a criminal's death by crucifixion!"

Love won then, and love still wins today.
Choose love.

Day 226

Put Your Hope in God

Nehemiah 7:73-9:21 / 1 Corinthians 9:1-18
Psalm 33:12-22 / Proverbs 21:11-12

As of August 2021, our world was still going crazy from the after-effects of the pandemic of 2020. The reports from our government were scary. Even the leaders of my home state of Tennessee were talking about things that might cause one's heart to fail them.

Our hope must remain in the Lord, especially during times when everything about our lives, including our ability to earn an income for our family and provide for them, is being threatened. I'm not sure when in history you will be reading this devotional, but the stories about 2020 and 2021 were real.

It's during times like these that I'm especially thankful for the book of Psalms. David, who wrote most of the Psalms, certainly understood difficult times and he was careful to write about his experiences so that we can receive courage from his writings today.

David didn't hold back. He spoke of the terrible things he endured, but he always came back around to speaking of the goodness of his God. We must follow this same pattern of overcoming fear and doubt and expressing our faith in God. That is the only way to thrive through difficult times.

The verses from Psalm 33 were very encouraging to read today! I will include them again here. Please read this passage and allow these verses to "put courage in you"!

"Blessed is the nation whose God is the LORD, the people He chose for His inheritance. From Heaven the LORD looks down and sees all mankind; from His dwelling place He watches all who live on earth – He who forms the heart of all, who considers everything they do."

"No king is saved by the size of his army, no warrior escapes by his great strength. A horse is a vain hope for deliverance, despite all its great strength it cannot save. But the eyes of the LORD are on those who fear Him, on those whose hope is in His unfailing love, to deliver them from death and keep them alive in famine."

"We wait in hope for the LORD; He is our help and our shield. In Him our hearts rejoice, for we trust in His holy name. May Your unfailing love be with us, LORD, even as we put our hope in You."

Take courage. Be strong. Have hope. The Lord your God is with you.

Day 227

Overcome Evil with Love

Nehemiah 9:22-10:39 / 1 Corinthians 9:19-10:13
Psalm 34:1-10/ Proverbs 21:13

We do not earn our salvation. We do not earn God's favor by the things we do after we have received the gift of salvation. However, we are expected to "work" in God's Kingdom.

We have a function in the body, gifts to operate in, and disciplines to acquire. There are certainly things to do, but none of the things we do will ever negate what Jesus Christ has already done. What He has done is our foundation upon which to build.

While we work for God, we must have the proper perspective of our work. Are we working to earn something, or are we working because we know we are loved, and we are grateful for all God has done? If for the latter, our work becomes a labor of love for God, and this is the best kind of labor in which we can engage.

1 Corinthians 9:26 is fascinating to me, especially when we read this verse in context of the verses both before and after. I'll quote verse 26 for you here, but please feel free to read the rest of the verses from today's devotional.

"So, I run with purpose in every step. I am not just shadowboxing."

Over the past several months, since I began my journey of reading the Bible through in a year and posting a daily blog, I've been aware that I wanted both to bring you something of value and to internalize for myself the truths I'm finding. If I study only to bring you a word, I've missed half of the point of studying. However, if I first search to find God's heart for me each day and I share with you out of that overflow, I believe my priorities are in line with God's purpose for my study.

Paul, the writer of the letters to the Corinthians, understood that he was not just teaching and training the early Christians. He knew that he was first a disciple or learner. He knew that his relationship with Christ was foremost. In a very real way, if a leader is studying God's Word just to preach a message that doesn't change his or her own heart, he or she is "shadowboxing".

To shadowbox is to punch the air without making contact. You've seen the movies of the prize fighter in training and he's making motions in the air with his gloved hands. It's true that he's gaining a measure of exercise through this and that without his training, when the real fight comes, he won't be able to withstand or have any chance of winning. Training is valuable (verses 24-25), so that we can stand when the battle begins.

In truth, we are in a battle daily. The enemy, the devil, is always pursuing us in an attempt to steal from us, kill us, and destroy everything God wants to do in our lives. That's why we can never afford to shadowbox.

We must be targeted and purposeful, hitting the mark often. We cannot accomplish this targeted campaign without Holy Spirit. He knows our enemy better than we do, and He can direct us toward the best methods for defeating the one who is attempting to defeat us.

Our greatest weapon in the Kingdom of God, the Kingdom of Heaven, is the love of God poured out through us onto those around. Do you want to defeat the enemy? Love others. Do you want to win the war? Guard your thoughts and your heart. Do you want the upper hand on every scheme the devil tries? Forgive everyone who has ever or will ever offend you.

We do not fight with weapons the way the world does. I feel like I should write that sentence one hundred times, so I remember it. I'm sure you remember writing sentences in school or at home. It was frustrating but it sure drove home the point of what you were writing.

How about this sentence, "I will not fight with weapons the way the world does? I will not speak evil things about others. I will not pay back evil for good or evil or evil."

This world is crazy and in desperate need of Jesus Christ. And that's where we step in. We who are filled with God's Spirit are meant to fill and permeate the atmosphere around us with the fragrance of Jesus. Don't stink up the place with pride, hatred, or any other evil-hearted thing! Repent and have a heart of love toward God and people. Remember, love is our greatest weapon.

If we have any hope of defeating the enemy in this hour, we must stand arm-in-arm with those we love and are in community with and declare the love of Jesus Christ over the entire earth! We must declare victory on His behalf. We must refuse to listen to the evil speakers of our day, and we must instead stand on the truth of God's Word. It is our only hope.

Day 228

Do What is Best for Others

Nehemiah 11:1-12:26 / 1 Corinthians 10:14-33
Psalms 34:11-22 / Proverbs 21:14-16

What if me, myself, and I chose to worship at the church of "my way", "doing what makes me feel good", and "don't tell me what to do"? Does that sound far-fetched? Well, outwardly it certainly does but how many of us live this way inwardly? We may not be aware of our motives, but our choices prove what is lurking within our hearts.

From birth we are conditioned to take care of ourselves first, and there is an element of that being necessary because if I'm not healthy and my needs are not being met, I will fall short in helping others. Once I'm strong enough, I need to put others first. I don't need to just think about putting them first; I need to do the work of putting them first.

> "I, too, try to please everyone in everything I do.
> I don't just do what is best for me; I do what is best for others
> so that many may be saved." — 1 Corinthians 10:33

The Passion Translation says it this way, "Follow my example, for I try to please everyone in all things, rather than putting my liberty first. I sincerely attempt to do anything I can so that others may be saved."

The Living Bible reads, "That is the plan I follow, too. I try to please everyone in everything I do, not doing what I like or what is best for me but what is best for them, so that they may be saved."

Do you know what I find interesting about these three translations? They all say the same thing. Others are first and I am second. Why? We deny ourselves and put the needs of others first so that the others in our lives may know Christ Jesus, and be born again. That certainly seems like a worthy cause. If I'm going to deny myself, I'd rather affect eternity in the process.

I've found that if I'm looking out for others, my needs will not go unmet; the Lord is taking care of me while I'm taking care of others. Part of the way He does that is through our faith communities. If the two concepts of taking care of yourself before taking care of others, along with putting others first is confusing, I understand! It certainly can be.

The heart of the matter is our heart motivation for why we do what we do. This is certainly not an easy, straight-forward topic. There are times I will tell others, "No," for the sake of being sure I stay sharp and focused, and there are times I'll spend myself beyond what feels like my breaking point because there is someone in need. And there will also be everything in between these two scenarios.

I've said for years that I will not be the person standing on the railroad tracks trying to stop a runaway train. That is valid. If someone finds themselves in a circumstance of their own making and they are not willing to cooperate with my help, it may be that they are not yet ready, and they are not yet miserable enough to change.

Then there are those who cannot help themselves in a particular circumstance and they just need someone to advocate for them. I will do that on a temporary, case by case basis. The key is being led by the Holy Spirit as we reach out to others.

At some point all of us must stand up and be big boys and girls and face the decisions we've made. Bad decisions make for bad outcomes. Wise decisions make for wise outcomes.

Those who are willing to do the hard work in their lives will reap the benefits. Those who do nothing except depend on others will find themselves not living the life they wished for. Therefore, let's encourage others to do their own hard work.

In summary, be strong, help others, and use wisdom according to what you hear Holy Spirit saying. Don't allow yourself to become cynical. Do what is best for others so that many may be saved.

Day 229

Allow the Lord to Build Your Walls

Nehemiah 12:27-13:31 / 1 Corinthians 11:1-16
Psalms 35:1-16 / Proverbs 21:17-18

The topic of walls is fascinating. I'm not referring to physical walls, but to walls we build to protect ourselves from being hurt emotionally. When we build walls in our hearts, we must realize that they are great at keeping things either inside or out.

There are times when the walls we've built are keeping out the good things God wants to bring into our lives. There are also times when those walls keep in the evil things the devil would like to use against us. It's important we're aware of which things we're keeping in and which things we're keeping out.

While learning about inner healing, I studied stronghold patterns and walls we've built in our hearts. The trouble with our personal walls is we're trying to protect ourselves when God wants to be the One who protects us. The walls we build put us in danger of stopping the flow of God's Spirit. God's walls of protection are more permeable and discerning, allowing Him full access to our hearts.

If we'll allow God to protect us, He will be the One to decide what gets in and out past the barrier He has around us. He knows what we need, and He knows what will harm us. We are not always fully aware of which things are for our best and which are attempting to harm us.

As I read about the completion of the walls around Jerusalem in Nehemiah, the leaders of Judah, and the two large choirs who climbed to the top of the wall, many thoughts about walls came to mind.

I was reminded about the verse in Psalm 125:2. That verse reads,

"Just as the mountains surround Jerusalem,
so the LORD surrounds His people, both now and forever."

Reading these words causes me to feel safe in the Lord's care. And I'm sure there was a measure of feeling safe as the walls and gates of Jerusalem were repaired in Nehemiah's time. This was an instance where walls were necessary for the protection of God's people.

When I read about two choirs walking along the wall singing in celebration, I wondered how wide and high those walls must have been. That's quite a large group. What kind of wall would have supported that crowd? So, I did a little research, and here's what I found.

The walls of Jerusalem were probably about 40 feet high and 8 feet wide, so there was plenty of space for a choir to walk in both directions until they met again at the other side. It's difficult to be sure exactly what the wall might have looked like, but some of the depictions I've seen indicate a parapet would have been included along the upper part of the wall. That would have been for safety and defense.

I've often wondered what it would have been like to be present during the times we read about in the Bible. Sometimes we think only about victories, but we must also consider the difficulties the people faced. I've often thought about how fascinating it would be to visit Israel and place my feet on the paths that those in scripture walked. Maybe that will be a reality one day.

But for now, I will enjoy reading the history and remembering that God is the same now as He was then. He is a God who still cares for, protects, and instructs His people today. And He is surrounding us now just as He surrounded those ancient walls in the days of Nehemiah. We are blessed that He does not change!

Day 230

Examine Yourselves

Esther 1-3 / 1 Corinthians 11:17-34
Psalms 35:17-28 / Proverbs 21:19-20

Have you ever studied the difference between the words "condemnation" and "conviction?" It is an important study because the misunderstanding of these two words will make the difference in your confidence in moving forward in your relationship with God, or in your coming to a standstill in great confusion. I do not wish for you to be confused or stopped in your forward movement with the plans God has for you! So, let's do a little study of words.

The word "condemnation" according to the Merriam Webster Dictionary is "to censure or blame." For further clarification the definition of the word "censure" is "to find fault with and criticize."

The definition of the word "conviction" is "the state of being convinced of error or compelled to admit the truth."

Based on these two definitions and combined with my own thoughts, my personal definition of the two words is as follows: condemnation is feeling guilt with no means of resolution, and conviction is feeling guilt with a clear path toward a solution to the problem at hand.

I believe the enemy of our souls, the devil, is king of condemnation because he enjoys making us feel horrible about ourselves and stopping us in our tracks so that we are unable to follow God's desires for us. Conversely, our loving God will bring conviction by the Holy Spirit, knowing He has already made a way for us to walk through the situation.

This reminds me of the verse in 1 Corinthians 10:13 which reads, "The temptations in your life are no different from what others experience. And God is faithful. He will not allow the temptation to be more than you can stand. When you are tempted, he will show you a way out so that you can endure."

Our Father does not want us stuck "in our feelings" with no escape. He sees the beginning, the middle and the end of every scenario we will ever face, and He has a path that will be best for us every time.

There are some things we can do to avoid the pitfalls of condemnation and judgment. We don't have to be trapped by either of these if we stay aware of our attitudes and actions and keep them aligned with scripture.

1 Corinthians 11:31-32 reads, "But if we would examine ourselves, we would not be judged by God in this way. Yet when we are judged by the Lord, we are being disciplined so that we will not be condemned along with the world."

It's interesting that verse 31 tells us to examine ourselves. If we are proactive enough to look at our own hearts – and doing so in prayer under Holy Spirit's guidance is best – we can avoid temptations and traps. I'm not saying we'll avoid every single temptation or trap, but we can certainly win more than we lose!

Scripture tells us in Jeremiah 17:9 Amplified Version, "The heart is deceitful above all things, and it is extremely sick; who can understand it fully and know its secret motives?"

The word "deceitful" is interesting because it can be defined as "slippery and hilly," making one believe the heart is deep and not easy to understand.

If we don't know our own hearts well, others certainly will not know our hearts and be able to help us navigate situations perfectly. Only Holy Spirit knows our hearts fully and can help us walk through the landmines we will face.

These facts lead me to believe that our only hope of successfully navigating through life's crazy situations is that we depend daily, hourly, and even minute by minute upon Holy Spirit. Father, Son and Holy Spirit are our lifelines in this walk of faith.

I have often stated that I don't understand how anyone makes it through life without help of some kind, and divine help is the best help. People mean well, and I'm thankful for them, but God's wisdom and insight far surpass anything a person can give me.

So, I'll keep my earthly relationships and remain grateful for those God has blessed me to be in relationship with. But I will also rely more heavily on God for the wisdom I need. I've been asking Him questions since I was old enough to talk and I haven't worn Him out yet! I'm confident I can keep asking questions for the rest of my life and He will always know what I should do!

147

Day 231

Another Runaway Train

Esther 4-7 / 1 Corinthians 12:1-26 / Psalm 36 / Proverbs 21:21-22

The story of Haman's demise would be comical if it weren't so sad and didn't end in his death. Even the death of an evil man is sad from an eternal perspective. It seemed that no matter what Haman tried, he was always one step behind his dark destiny. And the fact that he was completely unaware that he was falling into his own trap is especially devastating.

The first 4 verses of Psalm 36 perfectly describe Haman's character.

"Sin whispers to the wicked, deep within their hearts. They have no fear of God at all. In their blind conceit, they cannot see how wicked they really are. Everything they say is crooked and deceitful. They refuse to act wisely or do good. They lie awake at night, hatching sinful plots. Their actions are never good. They make no attempt to turn from evil."

Do you see what I mean? If you read Esther chapters 4-7 (and I hope you did!) those four verses in Psalm 36 appear to go hand in hand with Esther's account of Haman. He is so evil and deceived that he has no idea of what's coming. To think that there are people like that on earth may be obvious to some, but also incredible that they could walk in such deception.

I've wondered how another person can be so unaware of the evil they are perpetrating. In addition to the evil they pour out, they are totally oblivious that that same evil will come right back onto their own lives because of the spiritual law called sowing and reaping. What we put out to others is what we receive in return. There is nothing we can do to stop that reaping process, short of complete repentance.

I don't even know that repentance stops all the reaping process, because once a law is in motion, I don't know how long it takes to interrupt that process. God's grace can, of course, suddenly stop the backlash. But I've also seen and experienced a continuation of reaping what's been sown for a time. It's as if that runaway train I spoke of a few days ago needs a few more feet of track to come to a complete stop.

Sadly, Haman was impaled on the pole he set up to impale Mordecai. He literally died by the same means he had planned to kill an innocent man. I read of no repentance on his part, only pleading that he wouldn't be killed for his deception. As for you and me, I'm praying that we will quickly be made aware of our deceptions so that God's grace can cover us and save us from trouble.

I know it is God's heart to save and deliver us because we are His, and His mercy is great. The next verses of Psalm 36 are encouraging for those of us who are His. Let's look at those.

"Your unfailing love, O Lord, is as vast as the Heavens; your faithfulness reaches beyond the clouds. Your righteousness is like the mighty mountains, your justice like the ocean depths. You care for people and animals alike, O Lord. How precious is your unfailing love, O God! All humanity finds shelter in the shadow of your wings. You feed them from the abundance of your own house, letting them drink from your river of delights. For you are the fountain of life, the light by which we see."—Psalm 36:5-9

I want to end today's entry by considering those last five verses. They bring us around the other side of the circle of our thoughts. Instead of being stuck on the negative end of what happens with evil men and women, let's remember God's love and care toward us, even when we have been imperfect.

149

Day 232

Don't Allow Evil People to Make You Angry

Esther 8-10 / 1 Corinthians 12:27-13:13
Psalm 37:1-11 / Proverbs 21:23-24

I've talked a good bit about evil people, the craziness of our world and standing in faith instead of fear. And the world is still spinning out of control. However, our Heavenly Father is not spinning out of control. He is firmly and calmly seated on His throne and fully in charge of everything that is happening. We can't allow our hearts to be fearful based on what we see with our eyes; we must believe by faith that all will be well.

"Do not fret because of those who are evil."
—Psalm 37:1

Simple and to the point, this verse tells it like it is. I can certainly hear your questions and comments now. Yea, but evil people will always be here. We can't guarantee our own safety. What if my family or I are harmed? What if my needs are not met?

I totally understand these questions and comments, and I'm sure there are many others. I also will not pretend to have all the answers for you or for myself, but I know the One who does have answers.

Let's first dive into a little more information from the verse in Psalm 37. What does it mean to fret? We must know what the word means so we can choose not to do it! I've always thought the word "fret" referred to fear, but the meaning of the word from the Hebrew is "to be angry with, to be incensed, or to heat oneself with vexation." The word "vexation" is defined as "the state of being annoyed, frustrated, or worried."

So, while fear is certainly a part of the definition of the word "fret," it appears the meaning is more about anger, agitation, and frustration. And I have felt all these emotions many times in my life. I'm sure you have as well. Frustration usually sets in when there is something happening around us that we have no control over.

We may be aware of and see injustices all around us, but many times we feel there is absolutely nothing we can do to resolve the situation. Sometimes our legal system can step in and help, but many times apart from God's intervention, the injustice will continue. There are too many injustices to name, besides I don't want to head down a negative road by listing those here.

What about those who are evil? Who are they? They are people who produce injustice, evil, wickedness, violent deeds and wrong. We don't all know people like this, but they do exist. It's hard to fathom but there certainly are people in this world who love to do evil things just as much as we followers of Jesus love to do what is right.

We love what is right because of God's Spirit in us: those who do evil love what is evil because of the spirit of the demonic in them. There is a remedy for that if the person is willing to be free.

I'm thinking of a verse from Romans 12:21 that states, "Don't let evil conquer you but conquer evil by doing good."

Repaying someone who has done evil to us will just continue the evil storyline, but when we return good for their evil, they will either change their minds or walk away. Either response is a good one. I am not responsible for the way others behave; I am responsible only for my own behavior.

Day 233

Follow the Way of Love

Job 1-3 / 1 Corinthians 14:1-17 / Psalm 37:12-29 / Proverbs 21:25-26

When we love others, it is natural for us to want to give to and care for them. If we can relieve another's suffering, most of us would try to do our part, no matter how large or small. I believe most humanity is moved by the suffering of another. It is the rare person who is so evil he cares nothing for his fellow humans.

When we are secure in who we are now, and in who God has created us to be, we also do our best to elevate others toward being their best and finding their place in life. Each person has gifts, callings, and unique abilities. Some believe that if another has the same gift and they are both operating within the same space, one of them is not needed. I don't believe that.

Even if I have the same gift as another, the expression of that gift will vary based on personality and life experiences. I believe we are richer when we share and learn from one another, even when we find someone who is like us.

I enjoy sitting with someone who is artistic and experiencing the diversity of her gift. I also love being with another who is musically gifted and discovering how different their expression is from my own. And I enjoy sitting with people who are totally different from me, because I always learn something new.

I wish we all had this attitude of acceptance and love. Sadly, sometimes we treat each offering from another as a source of competition regarding our own expression. There is space for everyone to operate and give. Some have the mentality of scarcity and some the attitude of abundance. Those who think in terms of abundance enjoy all the expressions of others being shared, without feeling threatened.

1 Corinthians 14:1 is helpful.
"Follow the way of love and eagerly desire gifts of the Spirit."

Verse 3 says,
"But the one who prophesies speaks to people for their strengthening, encouraging and comfort."

We prove our love for others when we want to use our gifts to bless them. The blessings others receive from us include strength, courage, and comfort. I also believe that as we share our gifts, the giving bounces back into our own souls and we receive a blessing in return.

If each of us gives what we have, no one will lack anything. That's one thing I enjoy about a healthy church community; everyone comes with the attitude of giving away what they have to bless others. That way no one goes away empty. As a matter of fact, a true community of believers sharing together is one of the most satisfying and fulfilling experiences.

The next time you're preparing to meet with other Jesus followers, consider what you might bring of yourself to share with them. A smile, a hug, a song, a scripture, an encouraging word, a food item, anything really. Whatever it is you do well, bring that. Everyone will love the richness of their time together!

Day 234

No Spectators Allowed

Job 4-7 / 1 Corinthians 14:18-40 / Psalm 37:30-40 / Proverbs 21:27

Any time I'm with those who have different Christian traditions from mine, I begin considering the blessing of meeting together as followers of Jesus. The traditions are not what's important. It is the central truth around Jesus Christ that unites His followers.

The way we celebrate our faith is not as important as the fact that we recognize that Jesus Christ is the only way to the Father. If that truth is central, the forms for worship will vary widely but not take away from the foundation. Some love hymns, some choruses; some love kneeling for prayer and others love to stand; some enjoy raising their hands in worship and others enjoy keeping their hands quietly by their sides.

It makes my heart sad when I see others who name the Name of Christ criticizing differing forms of worship and gathering. I will say it again, it is not the forms, traditions, or ways we do things that make or break our faith; it is what we do with the sacrifice of God's Son that determines our Christian faith. Admittedly, our home church probably looks very different from other gatherings.

As a matter of fact, I've not experienced what we have before so we're heavily dependent on Holy Spirit to lead us each week into what He has in mind as we gather. Although we prepare and have a general flow in mind for our time together, we're always listening in case Holy Spirit has something He wants to say or do. We don't want to miss His plan for our time together!

1 Corinthians 14:26-31 describes well what we experience at Bethesda Springs House of Mercy and Grace when we get together. Here are those verses for you:

"Well, my brothers and sisters, let's summarize. When you meet together, one will sing, another will teach, another will tell some special revelation God has given, one will speak in tongues, and another will interpret what is said. But everything that is done must strengthen all of you.

"No more than two or three should speak in tongues. They must speak one at a time, and someone must interpret what they say. But if no one is present who can interpret, they must be silent in your church meeting and speak in tongues to God privately.

"Let two or three people prophesy, and let the others evaluate what is said. But if someone is prophesying and another person receives a revelation from the Lord, the one who is speaking must stop. In this way, all who prophesy will have a turn to speak, one after the other, so that everyone will learn and be encouraged."

I believe it is important that Father, Son and Holy Spirit are exalted and that the believers gathered go away feeling encouraged and filled with God. I also believe everything should be done with love and grace. Even if there is a need for redirection, that must be handled with humility and love. What does not matter is how these things are accomplished.

Jeff and I used to talk about how interesting it would be to visit other churches to see how different each one is. When we have visited other gatherings, I've experienced that each one will have a different personality. I believe that's because God is infinite in His expression and we as His people are expressing Him through our own unique gifts and life experiences. The body of Jesus Christ, which is the Church, is beautiful in her diversity and her unity.

The next time you gather with others who love Jesus Christ, consider what you might bring of yourself to give away so that those who are in attendance will be strengthened by you. Will you sing, share a scripture, or express a testimony? Or maybe you'll bring food or coffee? Or maybe God will tell you to bring a specific gift for someone or offer a specific service. Whatever God tells you to offer, be prepared to do so with confidence and a cheerful heart.

Day 235

You Can Learn the Easy Way

Job 8-11 / 1 Corinthians 15:1-28 / Psalm 38 / Proverbs 21:28-29

Have you ever tried to ignore a bully? They taunt, they laugh, they jab; they are just plain mean. If you can avoid giving them the time of day, they will eventually leave you alone. Bullies thrive on making people upset, and on getting a reaction to their irritating threats.

When my kids were little, and even still today, I told them to ignore it when others tried to irritate them. If someone is working to frustrate you and you don't give in, you've won! They will get tired of your lack of willingness to play the game, and they will move on. Don't get me wrong, you must have nerves of steel to ignore some people, but if you do, peace will reign.

Psalm 38:12-16 reads, "Meanwhile, my enemies lay traps to kill me. Those who wish me harm make plans to ruin me. All day long they plan their treachery. But I am deaf to all their threats. I am silent before them as one who cannot speak. I choose to hear nothing, and I make no reply. For I am waiting for you, O Lord. You must answer for me, O Lord my God. I prayed, 'Don't let my enemies gloat over me or rejoice at my downfall.'"

Not only is the Psalmist refusing to hear or respond, but he is also asking God to take care of the situation. Imagine the bully taunting you, and you withdrawing into the Spirit within you in prayer. Certainly, walk away, if possible, but try to find that place of peace in the Holy Spirit when outward irritations are threatening to make you say some not very nice words!

As one who loves to read, I have this habit of escaping into the world of whatever book I'm reading. As I escape, I'm not always aware of what's happening around me. When I was in middle and high school, I used to stay up late reading books, and I would imagine myself in the story. I would lose track of time and space as I became part of what I was reading.

There have been times when someone in my family is talking to me while I'm reading, and I don't even hear them until they touch my arm. What if we could somehow do that with the bullies? Not hear, not see, not even be aware that they exist. Truthfully, if they are that mean and antisocial, they probably could use some ignoring to perhaps wake them up to their evil ways!

Some people don't respond well or at all to corrections, so it becomes a waste of your breath and time to attempt to speak to them. Some of us need circumstances and consequences to smack us upside the head before we realize we need to change our behavior. I wish we could all learn lessons the easy way, but many prefer, by default, the hard road toward growth.

Which are you? Are you one who is humble and easily corrected, or are you stubborn, preferring to learn the hard way? I've heard people say they prefer to learn by allowing life to beat them up. Not me! I would much rather be humble, not easily offended, and able to learn when someone comes to me in love to share something that will help me grow.

As you do your personal assessment, if you find that you've been stubborn, repent and ask God to give you a pliable heart. None of us needs to be hard to teach or have difficulty learning the life lessons we need. We can always choose to be humble, learn quickly, and see major growth in our lives.

Day 236

Humility Brings Honor

Job 12-15 / 1 Corinthians 15:29-58 / Psalm 39 / Proverbs 21:30-31

It's important to give credit where credit is due. If you've done the hard work on a project, your name deserves to be highlighted so others will know your contribution. Many times, projects are worked on by a team of people which means the team will receive credit regardless of what part each member played.

As we work in our jobs, around our homes and in our churches, there is one credit we must remember to give and that is to God. The glory is forever and always His. We cannot do what we do unless He gives us His Spirit and help. We cannot accomplish any task unless He blesses us with the skills, gifts and talents needed. Every accomplishment must be credited back to Him because of His gifts and partnership in our lives.

James 1:17 confirms these thoughts. "Every gift God freely gives us is good and perfect, streaming down from the Father of lights, who shines from the Heavens with no hidden shadow or darkness and is never subject to change."

Since these gifts are streaming down from the Father, let's be sure we are prepared to walk in our calling. Speaking of preparation, our own hard work, and acknowledging God in all things, the following verse is a great reminder.

"The horse is prepared for the day of battle,
but the victory belongs to the LORD."—Proverbs 21:31

All the victory, the credit and the glory belong to the Lord, but that does not mean we are permitted to be lazy. We must plan, prepare, and do the hard work God has given us. We must be faithful and diligent to accomplish the tasks He puts before us.

Are you a business owner? Then manage your business and employees well, honoring God in your choices and showing love to the people around you. Are you a stay-at-home parent, responsible for your home and children? You must work just as hard as if you were outside the home and being paid by an employer. Why? Because you are employed for this calling by God, and He wants you to work at this job with all your heart as unto Him.

Are you employed by a company? You must work for that company with integrity, giving them your best while on the clock. After all, you not only want to earn a living to support your family, but you also want to honor God's Name in your work. If I haven't covered your situation, I believe what I have covered will give you an idea of faithfulness in your work.

How does that equate with being prepared for battle? Most of us will never "go off to war" or face physical battles, but we do face human and spiritual battles, and we must be prepared to stand strong in every situation. Planning, preparation, good use of our time, treasure, and talents – all of these are important.

Have you ever met a lazy person who would not work, plan, or prepare? It is right for that person to suffer loss and lack, even though that hurts our hearts to watch. Hard work and preparation certainly do pay off. But again, the victories in our lives belong to the Lord because He is the One who has given us all things.

When we're praised for something we've done well, it is right to receive the praise with thanks. However, do not forget to turn around and thank the Lord for His gifts that allowed you to show up well. This line of thought reminds me of another verse.

"I am the LORD, that is my name; my glory I give
to no other, nor my praise to idols."
—Isaiah 42:8 New Revised Standard Version

God is not in the habit of sharing His glory (honor, reputation). He is God and His being is unlike any other. We are not able to receive the honor that belongs to God. It would ruin us. That is what Lucifer wanted – God's glory for himself – and it destroyed him.

To sum up: planning and preparation are important. After having sought counsel from God, always be ready for whatever comes your way, armed with the wisdom He gives. When you receive praise for something you've done well, respond with humility. Be thankful for the praise but remember where everything you have comes from.

If we handle the credits and praises in our lives this way, we will do well. I also believe God will promote us, giving us more responsibility because He will know He can trust us. With promotions, stay humble. With increase in wealth, stay humble. With praise from others, stay humble.

Day 237

Wealth or Friendship?

Job 16-19 / 1 Corinthians 16 / Psalm 40:1-10 / Proverbs 22:1

I love to study the meanings of names. Our name meaning is filled with destiny and purpose, and I don't believe they are randomly chosen. I believe God places names on the hearts of our parents because He knows who He has purposed for us to be and the things He intends for us to accomplish.

A good name would also refer to our reputation, which is something we must build over time. A good name is not something we automatically have; it is something we must work to earn. My husband has been a contractor since 2000 and it has taken him many years to build his reputation to the point that when his name is mentioned, many people know that he will do good work.

Whatever your industry or ministry, you must work hard to be honest, filled with integrity, kind and many other adjectives that would honor both yourself and the Name of Christ. We don't work only for our own reputation; we also work for the reputation of Jesus in the earth. As followers of Jesus, we are upholding not only our own names, but also His Name.

"A good name is more desirable than great riches;
to be esteemed is better than silver or gold."—Proverbs 22:1 says

Your good reputation takes time to build and cannot be done apart from intimate relationships with others, whether in business or personal. If you do good work, that's valuable, but if you make others feel wanted and valued, that is of more value to them and to God. Good work may also open the door for opportunities to share the message of the Gospel of God's Kingdom.

Therefore, always do good work, remembering that others are watching to be sure your character matches what you've spoken. Remember also that it is not what we say that carries weight; our actions carry weight in the eyes of those watching. If you say one thing and do another, the thing you do will carry greater weight than your words.

Wealth, money, houses, farms, etc. are all blessings from God but if you have all that and cannot be trusted, what do you really have? To be esteemed means to have favor in the eyes of others. None of us wants wealth that comes with loneliness. I would rather have rich relationships along with having all my needs met than be wealthy beyond measure and live a solitary life.

No one truly wants to be alone, even the most extreme introvert craves human interaction. The only person who angrily states they want to always be alone is one who has been hurt and has not been able to forgive those who hurt her or him. Human kindness does more than fill our hearts, it heals our soul and body. We need that connection with others.

What can you do today to continue to build your good name? Or, if you've damaged your good name, what can you do to begin the process of repairing your reputation? Ask God for your next steps and get to work right away! You will never regret building a good reputation.

Day 238

Turn Around and Give it Away

Job 20-22 / 2 Corinthians 1:1-11 / Psalm 40:11-17 / Proverbs 22:2-4

When I don't feel well, or I've had a bad day or a loss of some kind, the last thing I'm considering is taking care of or encouraging someone else. Sometimes we can get so wrapped up in our own difficulties that we forget there are those all around us who need support. When one is in leadership, there is not always an opportunity to properly process our own situation before there is a need for us to jump into support mode for someone else we love.

> "He comforts us in all our trouble so that we can comfort others.
> When they are troubled, we will be able to give them the same
> comfort God has given us."—1 Corinthians 1:4

God is our comfort, especially when we are feeling alone or overwhelmed. What does the word "comfort" mean? Does it mean a hug? A listening ear? A meal brought, or sitting quietly together when someone feels alone? Let's look at the word because I'm wondering if there is not some sort of strength that is brought when the Lord comforts us, then compels us to turn around and comfort another.

The word "comfort" means "to call to one's side, to speak to with exhortation, entreaty, comfort, instruction, etc. To console, encourage, strengthen. To instruct or teach."

It turns out I was on the right track with the meaning of the word. As I read the definition, I had an understanding that comfort comes when we choose to be in close relationships with others. True comfort may come as a one-time offering, but I believe it is more effective when employed in the context of spending time in long-term friendship and love.

I've said it before and I'll say it again, "Loving others is hard work." It takes work to be in a relationship. Some want to be available only for the highs, not the lows, the ups, not the downs. But those in true relationship over many years will embrace every season. We will embrace the "warts" and the beauty of those we love. We will love them when they are easy to get along with and when they are difficult.

To do this, we must learn to walk in forgiveness and to see others through the eyes of Jesus. His perspective always gives a better picture. We usually see only the outward things of a person unless Holy Spirit helps us discern otherwise. And even with that discernment, we see only part of the story.

Let's also not forget that when we are feeling weak or low, we receive encouragement when we reach out to support and encourage someone else. Not only am I giving what I have received, I'm receiving as I give!

Acts 20:35 tells us, "And I have been a constant example of how you can help those in need by working hard. You should remember the words of the lord Jesus: 'It is more blessed to give than to receive.'"

When life is hard, instead of withdrawing into yourself and forgetting others exist, try reaching out to someone in need. I believe you'll find yourself strengthened and encouraged, and your problems may even look a little smaller or more distant. When you have received something from someone, remember to turn around and give to someone else when you have an opportunity. You will never regret the time you spend giving to others!

Day 239

Jesus Christ is Our Amen

Job 23-27 / 2 Corinthians 1:12-2:11 / Psalm 41 / Proverbs 22:5-6

I know you've met that person who is indecisive or insecure, and perhaps several other "ins" could be used to describe them. Maybe you've also been that person who has a hard time deciding, especially when you have a choice between two very good options.

As a quick decision-maker myself, I tend to get frustrated with those who waver. I'm aware I could make a wrong choice, but after I've considered, prayed, and asked for wise counsel, I would rather make a choice and move on. Otherwise, I start to feel stressed.

"For Jesus Christ, the Son of God, does not waver between 'Yes' and 'No.' He is the one whom Silas, Timothy, and I preached to you, and as God's ultimate 'Yes,' he always does what he says. For all of God's promises have been fulfilled in Christ with a resounding 'Yes!' And through Christ, our 'Amen' (which means 'Yes') ascends to God for his glory.'" —2 Corinthians 1:19-20

Of course, God would not waver between a yes or no answer. Jesus Christ, who is also God, will not waver when a decision is required. It's interesting to me that verse 19 calls Jesus, "God's ultimate yes". It's also interesting that all of God's promises were fulfilled in Christ with a resounding "Yes!"

Our "amen" or "yes" goes up to God for His glory. I think we need a word study and some additional context for these two verses to gain a little more information. Here is some history behind these verses.

Paul, Silas, and Timothy were the three men who established the church in Corinth, Greece. After establishing the church, all three men moved on in their journeys, presumably leaving the church in the hands of capable men. However, after their departure others came in whose teachings caused the church to question Paul's apostolic authority over the church.

In the context of these verses, it appears that among other issues, Paul's ability to keep promises is being questioned because he changed his mind about a visit. It's hard to find exact information from reading commentaries so some of this is supposition. If Paul's character is being called into question, he is willing to take this to task by reminding those he taught that the message and the messenger would have been one and the same.

If Paul's message was that God's promises could be fully trusted and realized through Jesus Christ, it would be assumed that those who brought the message could also be trusted. When the text states that God's promises are "Yes!", it is telling us that there is a strong affirmation and certainty behind this word.

If the promises of God are "yes" and "amen" in Jesus Christ, it's important we know what Jesus said of Himself. He was the first and the last, the beginning and the end, the Alpha, and the Omega. All things begin and end with Him, and those things which He has begun in us will be completed by Him. (See Philippians 1:6).

We can trust God, His Son Jesus Christ and His Word given to us in scripture. Yes, it is right for us to watch the life and character of the men and women who are bringing teachings to us from God's Word. If the character does not match the message, don't necessarily throw out the message (unless it is also false), but do consider what to do with the messenger.

We certainly want to submit ourselves to leaders who hold the utmost integrity in life because who they are will influence who we become. If we want to maintain an honest life, we must be led by those who lead an honest life. We really are affected by and become like those who mentor and teach us. So, choose wisely when choosing who you will allow to speak into your life. I would dare to say that having the Apostle Paul speaking into our lives is well worth the time!

Day 240

Church Rise Up!

Job 28-30 / 2 Corinthians 2:12-17 / Psalm 42 / Proverbs 22:7

No one wants to be on the losing team. You've heard the saying that it doesn't matter whether you win or lose, it's how you play the game. Let's face it; everyone would rather win than lose! We don't want to be the loser or on the losing team.

In our current society where everyone gets a participation trophy, I believe we've forgotten how to battle and win. The segment of society that appears to have forgotten this the most is the Church.

Now, before you get upset, understand that I am not disrespecting the Church. This will, however, be a call for her to arise and stand strong in the power of Holy Spirit as is her right and inheritance in the Lord. Jesus died on the cross for our freedom from sin, sickness, and disease but we do not always live in that reality. I believe it's time for the church to be encouraged and strengthened as she is reminded who she is and to Whom she belongs.

"For husbands, this means love your wives, just as Christ loved the church. He gave up His life for her to make her holy and clean, washed by the cleansing of God's Word. He did this to present her to Himself as a glorious church without a spot or wrinkle or any other blemish. Instead, she will be holy and without fault."—Ephesians 5:25-27

Jesus Christ loves His Church so much that He gave His life for her. We have already been presented in the Spirit to the Father as a beautiful bride for Jesus. Now, it is our responsibility to learn who we are and what we've been given and to walk in that purpose and destiny. But what if we've forgotten who we are and what we've been given?

"O God my rock,' I cry, 'Why have you forgotten me? Why must I wander around in grief, oppressed by my enemies?' Their taunts break my bones. They scoff, 'Where is this God of yours?' Why am I discouraged? Why is my heart so sad? I will put my hope in God! I will praise him again—my Savior and my God!"—Psalm 42:9-11

My first question is, "Why is Jesus's Bride grieving and oppressed?" I understand there are times we will be overwhelmed and times when we will forget who we are, but we must encourage both ourselves and one another to rise in the grace and courage Jesus Christ died to give us! You've heard there is strength in numbers and that is very true. The Church must gather to strengthen and encourage one another before we are swept away by evil.

On this day in history many in the church are waiting for a man or even for God to come and rescue us from the evil all around us. I hate to tell you this but evil is not going away while we live on earth so we must learn to deal with it properly.

We have authority over every evil thing – sickness, disease, sin, demons, all of it. But we've forgotten our authority. We've forgotten that we are sons and daughters of the King of the universe. We've forgotten what He died to give us. So, let's remember!

He has given us authority. Luke 10:19:

"Look, I have given you authority over all the power of the enemy, and you can walk among snakes and scorpions and crush them. Nothing will injure you."

He has given us grace.

"From his abundance we have all received
one gracious blessing after another."—John 1:16,

He has given us protection. Ephesians 6:10-18,

"A final word: Be strong in the Lord and in his mighty power. Put on all of God's armor so that you will be able to stand firm against all strategies of the devil. For we are not fighting against flesh-and-blood enemies, but against evil rulers and authorities of the unseen world, against mighty powers in this dark world, and against evil spirits in the Heavenly places.

"Therefore, put on every piece of God's armor so you will be able to resist the enemy in the time of evil. Then after the battle you will still be standing firm. Stand your ground, putting on the belt of truth and the body armor of God's righteousness. For shoes, put on the peace that comes from the Good News so that you will be fully prepared. In addition to all of these, hold up the shield of faith to stop the fiery arrows of the devil. Put on salvation as your helmet, and take the sword of the Spirit, which is the word of God.

"Pray in the Spirit at all times and on every occasion. Stay alert and be persistent in your prayers for all believers everywhere."

I especially appreciate that last line reminding us to pray in the Spirit at all times, stay alert and be persistent. That's hard work but very necessary for our survival, especially now. When you forget these things, I pray the Lord reminds you. When your family member or friend forgets, I pray you will remind them.

Let's remind each other according to this final verse from Hebrews 3:12-13,

"Be careful then, dear brothers and sisters. Make sure that your own hearts are not evil and unbelieving, turning you away from the living God. You must warn each other every day, while it is still 'today,' so that none of you will be deceived by sin and hardened against God."

Day 241

A Whole New You

Job 31-33 / 2 Corinthians 3 / Psalm 43 / Proverbs 22:8-9

Have you ever wanted to be a better person? You've tried your hardest to do the right thing, and to love people without being angry, offended, or judgmental. It's hard. It seems no matter how much willpower we try to muster we can't seem to improve ourselves. What about a self-help course? Maybe that would work.

Or maybe not. No matter how hard we try, apart from the life of Jesus Christ in us, we cannot become better people. We are attempting to be better from the outside in, when what we need is to be better from the inside out. Unless a person's heart and motives change, she or he will not be able to maintain a better way of life. I wonder if New Year's resolutions would work? Nah, probably not.

2 Corinthians 3:16-18 gives a great picture of what is needed to truly change.

"But whenever someone turns to the Lord, the veil is taken away. For the Lord is the Spirit, and wherever the Spirit of the Lord is, there is freedom. So, all of us who have had that veil removed can see and reflect the glory of the Lord. And the Lord—who is the Spirit—makes us more and more like him as we are changed into his glorious image."

The veil spoken of in these verses is the law, which represents condemnation toward our sinful nature with no way of escape. Once we turn to the Lord, that veil of condemnation is removed, and freedom comes.

2 Corinthians 5:17, "This means that anyone who belongs to Christ has become a new person. The old life is gone; a new life has begun!"

There is your "better person." Or in other terms, one who has laid a new foundation upon which to build. "New person" in the Greek language refers to "a new kind, something unheard of." What you were before Christ is nothing like what you are after Christ. From the moment of new birth, we have a genuine opportunity to change, to make something new out of our lives.

Everything we were is gone; we are no longer that old person. We may still find ourselves thinking about our old lives, and we may even be tempted to go back to some of our old habits, but now we have power to say "no" to those old habits and sins. They no longer have the right to dictate who we are!

I'm thankful the veil of the law was removed and that we are now walking according to the Law of Love. I'm thankful for my new life, my new self, and I'm grateful to have the opportunity of being changed into His image.

The next time you are frustrated with your imperfections, remember what Jesus has done in giving you the ultimate self-improvement "course."

Day 242

Beautiful Clay Pots

Job 34-36 / 2 Corinthians 4:1-12 / Psalm 44:1-8 / Proverbs 22:10-12

How does one go about determining the value of something? If we're speaking of antiques, I've heard there are several criteria. The age, the condition, whether there is the original packaging, and how rare the item is, as well as a determination of how many of that item were made.

Valuing items may be a little simpler to do, especially since one can do a search for a similar item online and get an idea of the value. But how does one value people? We certainly can't look that "item" up online.

Perhaps I should state that question more clearly. I am obviously not telling you to place a monetary value on a person, though some people do such things. In my opinion, humans are of inestimable value. We are patterned after our Creator and the worth He places on us is not determined in dollars and cents.

Have you ever wanted someone in your life only for what they could give you, do for you, or gain for you? Not only is that dysfunctional, but it's also abusive. We must love people because they are people not because they can benefit our lives in any way. If I sense someone is using me instead of loving me, I'm going to distance myself from that relationship. I will not be used.

God, the creator of the universe loves us so much that He found a way to impart Himself into us. The God of Heaven, the One who is all-powerful and all-knowing, placed His Spirit inside dusty vessels, or clay jars. As I read 2 Corinthians 4:7, I imagined the life and light of God bursting forth out of us, knowing we cannot possibly contain His majesty.

"We now have this light shining in our hearts, but we ourselves are like fragile clay jars containing this great treasure. This makes it clear that our great power is from God, not from ourselves."—2 Corinthians 4:7

God has absolutely nothing to gain by placing Himself into human containers. The only "benefit" is that we gain life and peace through our Lord Jesus Christ, and anyone who receives this gift is made right with God and inherits eternal life. That sounds like we are the ones who gain all the benefits!

When verse 7 referred to us as fragile clay jars, that is when I imagined His light and life bursting out of us. However, for His light to emanate from us, we must allow some cracks, some breaking, some imperfections. Since we are already imperfect, if we'll embrace our imperfections, we are wonderful candidates for showing forth the glory of God.

That is part of why He fills us, so that we can show His glory in the earth, drawing others to the eternal life we carry. After all, wouldn't we want everyone to share in the life of Christ both here and in Heaven? That is God's heart in sending His Son to earth to live a sinless life, die on a cross, and rise again. God wanted to reconcile the ones He created to Himself through His Son.

We were once separated from our heavenly Father by sin, but we no longer need to live that way. A way has been provided for a restored relationship with God. It is amazing that God would want a relationship with us. Perfection loves imperfection. The sinless One loves those who were chained by sin.

The next time you're looking at a fellow human, remember that she or he was created by God as an object of love. He loves them regardless of how they behave or how they treat you or me. Remember, if she has received His Spirit, that clay vessel contains the life of God. Please treat her with love and respect.

Day 243

A Renewed Spirit

Job 37-39 / 2 Corinthians 4:13-5:10 / Psalm 44:9-26 / Proverbs 22:13

Sometimes my body is so achy that I'm ready to be healed or move to Heaven, but most of the time I'm excited about life here and the opportunity to live another day, loving Jesus and my people and helping others know Him more. I've heard that getting old isn't for sissies. At 60-something, I don't feel old yet, but like I said, my body sure is talking more and more as the years pass.

Part of my pain is due to a car accident in 2013 that caused a disc rupture and nerve damage. The rupture required surgery in March 2014, and let me tell you, nerves heal very slowly. The sciatic nerve in my right leg was severely damaged by the rupture but the Lord promised to heal me. I hold onto that promise of healing.

Like some of you, when low pressure weather systems enter our area, my body can tell. The past few days have been that way. It's August, so we're not too far away from full-blown hurricane season.

We're being affected now by a low-pressure system and rain from Hurricane Ida that wiped out Louisiana. Bradley's family (our son-in-law who passed away in January 2021) still lives there, and we've been praying hard for all of them as they suffer loss and hard times.

Did you know that from the moment we are born our physical bodies begin to die? I guess that sounds morbid, but it's true. We celebrate new life when a baby is born but from the moment we enter earth, our days have been counted by God. We have only a certain number and none of us knows how long we'll be here. Considering that fact, it's important to live each day looking to God's Spirit for His plan.

"That is why we never give up. Though our bodies are dying, our spirits are being renewed every day."—2 Corinthians 4:16

What is the "why" spoken of in that verse? The answer is found in verse 14. "We know that God, who raised the Lord Jesus, will also raise us with Jesus and present us to Himself together with you."

Even though we are counting our days left on earth, and even though our bodies are dying daily, we have this amazing hope of being raised with Jesus and presented to the Father. Now, before you think I believe we are just biding our time and waiting for the sweet by and by, let me assure you that I believe our inheritance is not in Heaven only. We have an inheritance here also.

"We also pray that you will be strengthened with all his glorious power so you will have all the endurance and patience you need. May you be filled with joy, always thanking the Father. He has enabled you to share in the inheritance that belongs to his people, who live in the light."—Colossians 1:11-12

We have a beautiful life and inheritance as we live in community with other Jesus followers. We also have a mandate to bring Heaven to earth every day. Are you working to do that?

Remember the part of the Lord's prayer that says, "On earth as it is in Heaven?" In Heaven everything is perfect and complete, and we can pray that completeness and perfection will impact our earthly experience.

Do you need healing? You are healed in Heaven! Do you need

salvation? Your salvation exists in Heaven through Jesus Christ. Do you need hope, joy, or peace? It's all available in the realm of God's Spirit.

Our spirits are being renewed every day by God's Spirit. All we must do is be aware, connect with Him through His Word and in prayer, and we have everything we need! Even if your body is screaming at you, your spirit man can be energized and excited about what God is doing.

That is the life I'm living, and I want to invite you to join me. How? By accepting Jesus Christ as your Savior and Lord and by submitting your life to him daily.

> "If you openly declare that Jesus is Lord
> and believe in your heart that God
> raised him from the dead,
> you will be saved."—John 10:9.

Day 244

What is My Life Calling?

Job 40-42 / 2 Corinthians 5:11-21 / Psalm 45 / Proverbs 22:14

When you find your life calling the revelation of it may feel very "heavy." You may be filled with fear, doubt, excitement, and many other emotions. You will face persecution and resistance; it will be only the few who will receive you as God designed you. Why? Because you are a threat to them.

Why? Because, if you have found your path, that means there is a path to find. If others have not yet found their path, they will either be spurred to find it or will get angry at you for what you are doing that they are not.

It seems unfair, but it's human nature. The compelled ones cannot help but run and speak, while the lazy ones cannot find anything to compel them. I've often wondered why some are compelled and others sit idly watching from the stands.

What makes one a Caleb – the one with a different spirit who served God wholeheartedly? Why is it that only a few step into their calling, while others wander through life unsure of what God meant for them?

I believe it is because our enemy does not want us to know who we are, so he fights against us relentlessly. Some fight back while others are not aware that they may fight back because of their upbringing, past trauma, or their faith experience. Our enemy has been attempting to throw mud and cast shade on us since our conception. I'm sad to tell you this, but he hates you and wants to kill, steal from, and destroy you.

But there is good news! Greater is He that is in you than he that is in the world. GREATER is JESUS in you than the devil who thinks he rules anything or has the upper hand in any situation. There may be giants in the land, but Jesus Christ through the cross has given us complete and total victory! Once we see our victory, we have a mandate.

I have several favorite portions of scripture. Isaiah 61 is a life mandate for me. I also really love Romans 8. But when I read 2 Corinthians 5:11-21 I have a hard time staying in my skin. This is my life's calling. Let me put those verses here so you can read them. The title of this portion of scripture is "We Are God's Ambassadors."

"Because we understand our fearful responsibility to the Lord, we work hard to persuade others. God knows we are sincere, and I hope you know this, too. Are we commending ourselves to you again? No, we are giving you a reason to be proud of us, so you can answer those who brag about having a spectacular ministry rather than having a sincere heart. If it seems we are crazy, it is to bring glory to God. And if we are in our right minds, it is for your benefit. Either way, Christ's love controls us. Since we believe that Christ died for all, we also believe that we have all died to our old life. He died for everyone so that those who receive his new life will no longer live for themselves. Instead, they will live for Christ, who died and was raised for them."

"So, we have stopped evaluating others from a human point of view. At one time we thought of Christ merely from a human point of view. How differently we know him now! This means that anyone who belongs to Christ has become a new person. The old life is gone; a new life has begun!"

"And all of this is a gift from God, who brought us back to himself through Christ. And God has given us this task of reconciling people to him. For God was in Christ, reconciling the world to himself, no longer counting people's sins against them. And he gave us this wonderful message of reconciliation. So, we are Christ's ambassadors; God is making his appeal through us. We speak for Christ when we plead, 'Come back to God!' For God made Christ, who never sinned, to be the offering for our sin, so that we could be made right with God through Christ."

There is not enough space to speak about each of these verses, because I prefer to keep these entries short for your sake. However, I will bring out one sentence, maybe two!

He died for everyone so that those who receive His new life will no longer live for themselves. If I have received His new life, I will not live for myself. I will live to rescue and restore others who have not yet seen and received what I have seen and received. After all, isn't this the one message that matters most!

God has given us this task of reconciling people to Him. There it is. If you do not know your calling, this is at least part of it! We already have eternal life. We already have Jesus Christ. We are already daughters and sons of the King.

What about our fellow man and woman? Who will speak to them? Who will rescue them? You may say, "It is God's job to rescue." And you are correct. However, He does that rescue operation through you and me.

We are at war. I encourage you to find your post, arm yourself with God's Word and Spirit and hold fast. Do not waver, do not be fearful because the Lord your God is with you wherever you go.

Day 245

Weapons, Walls and Foundations

Ecclesiastes 1-3 / 2 Corinthians 6:1-13 / Psalm 46 / Proverbs 22:15

If you're a builder in God's Kingdom, you understand the need to build, defend and attack all at once. If that sounds exhausting, keep in mind that when we join the Father in His work, we are resting from our own work. Remember also that His yoke is easy, and His burden is light. (See Hebrews 4:9-10 and Matthew 11:29-30)

In 2 Corinthians 6:7, what does it mean that we use the weapons of righteousness in the right hand for attack and the left hand for defense? As a builder, Nehemiah understood both attacking and defending while he led the people in rebuilding the walls of Jerusalem.

We attack with the right hand by using our sword, which is the word of God. We defend with our left hand as we hold our shield of faith in front of us. If you're left-handed, you would switch which hand holds each item. While we're attacking and defending, we are also building. What does it look like to build?

The Kingdom of God is built differently from the kingdoms of earth, although some concepts are the same. Both kingdoms have foundations and walls that can be built with blocks, bricks, stones, and mortar. When we compare, our Kingdom foundation is Jesus Christ; an earthly foundation is made of concrete and steel rebar.

A Kingdom wall is built with "living stones" who are the body of Christ built together; an earthly wall is made from bricks or stones with mortar.

I mentioned "living stones" in the previous paragraph. If we as Kingdom builders are building with "living stones", what might that look like? First, the stones must be of good quality, meaning we must learn to properly care for, equip and activate each person God brings to us. Next, we must model what it looks like to be joined to the other stones so that our wall will be strong.

I believe it is the Holy Spirit who acts as mortar in joining us together as stones to create a beautiful wall. Therefore, we must learn to invite, honor and follow Holy Spirit as He leads us, and we must teach others to do the same. As we grow together, the rough edges of each stone will become polished so that we fit together to create a stronger bond and therefore a stronger building.

I love Jude 1:20-21 which reads,

"But you, dear friends, must build each other up in your most holy faith, pray in the power of the Holy Spirit, and await the mercy of our Lord Jesus Christ, who will bring you eternal life. In this way, you will keep yourselves safe in God's love."

Final thoughts on weapons, walls and foundations. We must remember that the weapons we fight with are not like earthly weapons, but they are instead used to war in the Spirit. Spirit weapons include prayer, worship and love for one another. Walls in the Spirit realm are alive because they are formed through the connection of people. And foundations? We have just one, and His name is Jesus Christ.

Give careful thought to how you build using the tools and materials God has supplied. When your life is complete, if you have used His tools and materials, your work will survive that final testing by fire. (See 1 Corinthians 3:13)

Day 246

Weigh Your Trust Carefully

Ecclesiastes 4-6 / 2 Corinthians 6:14-7:7 / Psalm 47 / Proverbs 22:16

Depending on others can be a tricky business. Everyone has seasons of strength and seasons of weakness. We're taught in Christian circles to depend on God first, then ask people to partner with us. However, we must never fully depend upon or put our trust in people because people are weak and finite in their wisdom and strength.

In much of the reading today I was reminded to be cautious regarding who I put my trust in. I'm not speaking of basic trust of God and people; I'm speaking of placing too much weight on humanity, especially the wicked or those who care nothing about right living before God. If you trust the wrong person or thing, you may find yourself burned or ruined before you even know what hit you.

> "Those who love money will never have enough."
> —Ecclesiastes 5:10

I'm reminded of many today who care only for money and things and sadly care nothing for the people around them. Don't make the mistake of trusting someone like this. However, if you find someone to trust or count on, that will be to your advantage.

I love the verses in Ecclesiastes 4:9-12:

"Two people are better off than one, for they can help each other succeed. If one person falls, the other can reach out and help.

But someone who falls alone is in real trouble. Likewise, two people lying close together can keep each other warm. But how can one be warm alone? A person standing alone can be attacked and defeated, but two can stand back-to-back and conquer. Three are even better, for a triple-braided cord is not easily broken."

It's who you choose to trust that makes the difference. We are warned in 2 Corinthians 6:14, "Don't team up with those who are unbelievers. How can righteousness be a partner with wickedness. How can light live with darkness?" Discernment is a key need among believers; don't be fooled by words but seek wisdom from God's Spirit before committing yourself to any situation.

Unfortunately, Jeff and I have learned this the hard way. For example, we may find someone who claims the name of Christ, and decide to partner with them in business, community, or life. However, we must first take time to test their character and ask around regarding their reputation. We've been burned a couple of times thinking we were making a good partnership.

On another note, sometimes partnering with friends in business may not end well. I would rather have the friendship and stay at peace with one another than make a buck and end up as enemies. Money or friendship?

If you're in a situation simply for your own advantage, or you find yourself in a situation where the other person is only there for his or her own advantage, extricate yourself quickly. I'm speaking from experience. You may find yourself taken to court and you may lose more than you bargained for!

Do everything in love. And seek to partner with those who have the same value. I'm not saying you can't be friends with the lost or those whose values don't quite match your own, however, keep a safe distance until someone's character is proven.

Never rush into any relationship or situation. Take time to pray, asking God for His heart. I promise He'll guide you if you ask, seek, knock, and listen. You'll also be saved from much heartache by entrusting all your decisions to God.

Day 247

The Choice is Yours

Ecclesiastes 7-9 / 2 Corinthians 7:8-16 / Psalm 48 / Proverbs 22:17-19

Have you ever been sorry you got caught doing what you knew better than to do? Were you sorry you did it or sorry you got caught? There is a difference.

When I was in 9th grade my best friend Sheri lived down the street. We used to get snow when I was younger, now we rarely do. When it snowed, we had the most amazing time sledding on the hills on our street!

If we weren't sledding with the rest of our neighbors down the biggest hill in the subdivision in front of our house, we would be attempting a daredevil feat at Sheri's house. Sadly, one time that adventure didn't end well.

We would start in her backyard, head through the front yard, make a sharp right once we hit the street then another sharp right as the road turned. If you didn't make that last sharp right, you were going through a barbed wire fence into a cow pasture.

I'm sure you can figure out what happened the last time we tried that. Our parents warned us not to try this tricky maneuver, knowing that the fence might catch us if we missed that turn. But it was so much fun that we wanted to do it just one more time.

It took only one time to fly right through that fence ripping my brand-new winter down coat to shreds on the barbed wire. There was no sneaking into the house unnoticed that day. I knew what was coming.

Was I sad about my coat? Yes. Was I sad that I hadn't obeyed?

No. The thought of one more thrilling ride outweighed the possibility of getting caught. And caught I was, in more ways than one.

2 Corinthians 7:10 tells us:

"For the kind of sorrow God wants us to experience leads us away from sin and results in salvation. There's no regret for that kind of sorrow. But worldly sorrow, which lacks repentance, results in spiritual death."

If only I had listened. If only I hadn't taken that last ride. If only I had believed that my parents had wisdom for me that day. I would still have had my coat and wouldn't have had to walk home ashamed.

If only.

There was plenty of regret that day. I don't remember what my punishment was; it may have been the loss of my coat. I certainly did not sled that route again. I may even have been forbidden from sledding the rest of that day. Was the thrill of that last ride worth the trouble I gained? I don't remember how I felt about that either.

If I had the right kind of sorrow, I would have been led away from sin. Of course, this verse is speaking more of a sorrow that leads us toward Salvation. Much more is at stake in our turning from sin while turning toward God for salvation. But the small opportunities for obedience prepare us for the larger opportunities for obedience toward God.

We learn obedience from our parents as children so we will better obey God when we're grown. Or hopefully that is how it works. Our parents are attempting to train us for adulthood.

They don't want us to be adults who want nothing but our own way because they know the worthless places that will lead. They know that we will not be responsible adults unless we are willing to be under the authority of God. In that way, they are providing us a service.

Most of you are probably in the adult season of life, although maybe a younger person might be reading this devotional book. Wherever you are in life, I pray you have found the value of obedience, not simply to keep you out of trouble, but so that you will have true joy in life. There really is joy in listening to and following God along the path He knows is best for us.

You've heard the sayings, "Pick your poison", or "Pick your pain." I'm going to tell you to pick your obedience and therefore your consequences. Consequences are coming and they can be either fruitful good ones or negative ones that will suck the life out of you. It really is your choice.

I place before you today life and death; choose life. (See Deuteronomy 30:15)

Day 248

The Cage Door is Open

Ecclesiastes 10-12 / 2 Corinthians 8:1-15 / Psalm 49 / Proverbs 22:20-21

You may be shocked to hear that slavery still exists today, though not as it did in the past in our nation. There are still those sold into slavery of many kinds, and it is an ugly truth to consider. There is also spiritual slavery with which we must contend. Neither the physical nor the spiritual slave can free himself or herself. To be freed from slavery we need a benefactor or one who will be kind enough to pay for our release from this evil.

Most people would agree that physical slavery is evil. No human should own another human or use another human for any purpose. But do we see spiritual slavery in the same light? Slavery to the devil and to sin begins with the enslaving of our souls, but since we are affected physically by what happens in our souls, both are affected. How are we to gain freedom?

A way has been provided. A gift has been given. All we must do is turn our heads or our hearts toward the truth and we will find the path that has been made clear by Jesus Christ. He has certainly defeated the enemies of death, hell and the grave and we no longer need to feel threatened by that type of slavery. However, what if we still choose to be enslaved? That's a good question.

Apart from the Father drawing us, we cannot awaken to the love of the Father given through the Son (see John 6:44). Once we feel the drawing of the Father, or hear the calling of His voice, we have a choice to make. Will we listen? Or will we turn away? Will we receive His love, or will we reject His offered gift? The gift is rejected only when fear is present, causing us not to understand what is being offered.

There are no strings attached. We will not lose anything in saying, "Yes" to the gift of salvation – except our sorrow, sin, and slavery. That sounds like an excellent trade to me. Unfortunately, sometimes fear and lies form in our minds, and we turn away, unable to believe this gift doesn't come with certain expectations.

"But as for me, God will redeem my life. He will snatch me from the power of the grave."—Psalm 49:15

When we redeem something or someone, we buy them out of the situation they find themselves in. It's usually a helpless and hopeless state of mind and heart that keeps us in darkness. But a great light came. A great hope has shined into our hearts by Holy Spirit, allowing us to see that we can be free.

I love the wording above. "He will snatch me from the power." The word "snatch" is a forceful word, so I wanted to look at the original language to see if that same force was intended.

The Hebrew word for "snatch" means "to lay hold of, to seize, to take away." The word can also mean "to take in marriage." I find that to be interesting because once we belong to Christ, we are His bride in the spiritual sense.

Those in history who were sold into slavery were also seized. They were taken against their will and sold into a life no human should have to endure. Sin has attempted the same type of violent seizure upon our souls. God saw the attempted kidnapping and He determined to put a halt to the injustice perpetrated upon His beloved creation.

Make no mistake, this is not a tug-of-war game. The devil has attempted to seize us through sin, but now because of the sacrifice of

Jesus on the cross, the Father is making a countermove and seizing us again to Himself. We began as His and He has provided a way so that we may end as His.

This is a case where the end is most certainly better than the beginning. I'm thankful for His counterattack upon the kingdom of darkness. I'm thankful we are no longer slaves. I'm thankful we have seen that the door to the cage is open, and that we can walk through to the other side.

203

Day 249

Duplicate Yourself into Others

Song of Songs 1-4 / 2 Corinthians 8:16-24
Psalm 50 / Proverbs 22:22-23

When we leave the earth, each of us hopes that our name and good reputation will live on. We hope to be remembered for having been kind and generous, along with any other positive character trait one could think of. Unfortunately, not everyone will leave behind a positive legacy. Personally, one of my most fervent prayers is that the life I'm pouring into others will have a massive impact.

Some of those who are influenced by us will be so because they chose to listen, learn, and grow without us ever knowing we were having an effect. Others will actively seek a relationship and will let us know the impact we're having in their lives. All of us will have both types of people in our lives; those we know we've affected, and those we are unaware of.

Then there is a third option and that is a mentoring relationship. In a mentoring relationship, one hopes to teach the other person all they can with an expectation that the work begun will be carried into further effectiveness for God's Kingdom. As of this writing, I have not had one specific mentor in my life, though I'm confident the many relationships I've been blessed to engage in have helped me grow.

When I look at my children, I am aware that my discipleship of them will be a large part of the legacy I leave behind. They will in turn leave a legacy to their children, and so on. When Paul speaks of Titus in 2 Corinthians 8:16-24, the verses cause me to imagine how proud Paul must have been. In verse 16 he said, "But thank God! He has given Titus the same enthusiasm for you that I have."

I imagine that Paul felt a similar pride in Titus to what I feel in watching my adult children as they find their paths in life. Paul's statement about Titus seems to indicate they have spent a considerable amount of time together. I've heard it said that vision is caught and not taught. I believe that Titus has caught vision from Paul and is excited to continue the work of supporting the churches in the region.

Since we can't take anything with us when we leave earth, we are wise to leave behind a legacy that surpasses money and possessions. Instead of only bank deposits, let's prioritize making deposits into the hearts of those around us. That means we must commit to being in relationships with others.

Whose life are you impacting today? Hopefully you've begun to feed yourself so you can feed others. To love yourself so you can love others. To forgive yourself so you can forgive others.

I encourage you to fill up on God's Spirit first, then allow the overflow to help nourish others. Also, remember how important it is to teach others to feed themselves. We must eventually graduate from baby bottles to forks, spoons and sharp knives!

Day 250

The Magnifying Glass of the Father

Song of Songs 5-8 / 2 Corinthians 9 / Psalm 51 / Proverbs 22:24-25

When you're hanging out with family or friends, do you often wonder how well you really know a person's heart? We only reveal to others what we are comfortable revealing. Vulnerability is not an easy request or task.

If I share my fears or secrets, they could later be used against me. Does that mean I should keep all my secrets to myself? Not all, but we certainly should not share everything with everyone.

"The human heart is the most deceitful of all things, and desperately wicked. Who really knows how bad it is?"— Jeremiah 17:9

We don't even know the depths of everything within our own hearts, much less what is in the hearts of others. People only let us see what they want us to see. Some are very good at hiding their true thoughts and feelings from others. Some are open books, but probably still withhold their deepest, darkest secrets for fear if we really knew them, we would not love them.

Psalm 51:6 in the New American Standard Bible shows us what God desires for us. "Behold, You desire truth in the innermost being, and in secret You will make wisdom known to me."

"Truth in the innermost being." God sees what no one else sees. God knows what even we are not fully aware. There are twisty, dark places in our hearts that we have been too afraid to admit to ourselves and to God. However, He already knows, and He loves us anyway!

Our Father is aware that we are imperfect. Even if we tried to do everything right, looking good to the outside world, there would still be "stink" in our hearts. The good news is that He doesn't want us to remain deceived by those hidden places. So, in secret He wants to make wisdom known to us. "In secret" may be referring to that quiet place within our spirits where He speaks to us in love and brings His truth to set us free.

I also believe He has no desire to shame us, so He attempts to bring correction just between the two of us, hoping we will listen and change the way we think. God does not want to call us out publicly, hoping the embarrassment will cause us to want to do things differently. He wants to lead us in His gentle love toward a life that better reflects Jesus Christ.

That is our goal; to look like Jesus Christ. That is an effort which will take a lifetime to achieve. As a matter of fact, even in our final day, we will not have completed this work of looking like Jesus. But when we see Him face to face, we will have been made perfect because of His sacrifice on the cross. That will be a beautiful day!

Don't wait for the "beautiful day" to be made perfect. Seek to know and be like Him now. We don't pursue change because we want to be better; we pursue change because we love Him and want to please Him. On the one hand, the Father is already fully pleased with us because we are seen through His Son. On the other hand (third hand?), it is to our advantage to grow, change and mature.

If you imagine that Holy Spirit is looking into your heart for the next hidden area to be brought into the light, remember that this search is done in love. This search is done for your benefit and good. Allow Him to look because He is looking with love.

Day 251

Those in Authority

Isaiah 1-2 / 2 Corinthians 10 / Psalm 52 / Proverbs 22:26-27

Perhaps all of us have experienced abuses of one kind or another, some more damaging than others (though all abuse is damaging). There are many types of abuse, and I will not name them all because I don't want to cause you sorrow in remembering any of your own abuse. One abuse I will mention is that of power or authority. That is a wrong that has been perpetrated for centuries and one that we will not see the end of until this earth is made new.

2 Corinthians 10:8 was interesting to me, and I appreciated it as stated by Paul. It reads:

> "So even if I boast somewhat freely
> about the authority the Lord gave us
> for building you up rather than tearing you down,
> I will not be ashamed of it."

Not all authorities are Christian, but all authority is ordained by God, even the ungodly authorities around us. Why would God allow ungodly authority? We can look at our own nation and world and realize there is an awakening happening through the difficulty of some who are godless leaders. I believe God allows these hardships so they will cause us to turn our hearts back to Him.

We, like the people of Israel in the Old Testament, have turned our hearts away from following God and have become complacent. Sometimes trouble and persecution can jolt us to awaken, repent and restore our relationship with God. I pray this will happen for our world today.

Every person is subject to the governing authorities. Since there is no authority except from God, we as Christians must seek to honor those God has allowed to rule over us. That doesn't mean we blindly obey or that we dishonor God. (See Romans 13:1 New American Standard Bible).

> "It is He who changes the times and the periods;
> He removes kings and appoints kings;
> He gives wisdom to wise men, And knowledge
> to people of understanding."—Daniel 2:21

> "The nations will know that the house of Israel
> went into exile for their wrongdoing, because they
> were disloyal to Me, and I hid My face from them;
> so, I handed them over to their adversaries,
> and all of them fell by the sword."—Ezekiel 39:23

The verses above prove that God does place and remove leaders, as well as brings evil leaders into the scene to bring an awakening to His people when they have forgotten Him. But what about godly leadership, or those who claim the name of Christ, yet are still acting in an evil manner? That, sadly, also happens.

Paul was a godly leader with great integrity, and he was reaffirming that he was determined to use his authority to build up rather than tear down the Church. There are many good leaders in the Church today, but there are also leaders who are insecure and not quite prepared for the role they are fulfilling. We must not forget that those in leadership are held in stricter judgment by God and are accountable for the way they treat those they lead.

James 3:1, "Dear brothers and sisters, not many of you should become teachers in the church, for we who teach will be judged more strictly."

Even the Pharoah in Egypt in Moses's day, who was intended by God to be used to bring judgment on God's people, was later condemned for having touched God's people. Meaning, even the evil leaders will also reap where they have sown. This is a heavy topic, I understand. Abuse, evil leaders and judgment are not light subjects.

The good news is God is a good Father, and a loving leader. If we follow His voice, we will find ourselves under godly leadership. Pray for godly leadership so that your life will be peaceful.

1 Timothy 2:1-2, "I urge you, first of all, to pray for all people. Ask God to help them; intercede on their behalf and give thanks for them. Pray this way for kings and all who are in authority so that we can live peaceful and quiet lives marked by godliness and dignity."

If you find yourself under harsh leadership in the Church, ask God what He would have you do. He may want you to stay, or He may want to move you out. When it comes to national leadership, we have little choice but to stay and pray. Please pray for your nation and its leaders today!

Day 252

The Lord Fulfills His Own Word

Isaiah 3-5 / 2 Corinthians 11:1-15 / Psalm 53 / Proverbs 22:28-29

I've noticed something over the years that is disturbing. When someone dies, the family and friends of the deceased get a little weird about their possessions. I've seen squabbles, grabs for things someone has no right to, etc. It seems that instead of grieving as a priority, some are concerned with what they will gain by this person's passing.

In 1998 a family friend passed away. Myra and her husband Roy had been part of the church my daddy pastored. Myra came with her baggage, just like we all do, but she really was a precious lady. After the church was disbanded in 1984 and my parents moved to North Carolina in 1988, Myra would call me to talk and ask for prayer. I didn't understand why she had chosen me as a trusty ear, but she did.

In 1998 I was receiving the occasional call as usual. I would pray for her, encourage her and love her as best I could. When I went through my divorce in 1985, I lived with Myra for a few months during my transition. She had been very kind to me, taking me in during a time of need.

In the fall of 1998, we were called to visit her in her hospital room and asked to bring all her earrings so she could choose a favorite pair. I didn't realize that she had been told she was dying.

Jeff and I went to visit, taking all her earrings as requested. When we arrived, her lawyer was also present. There was some paperwork that we were being asked to sign because Myra wanted us to execute her will when the time came. I just didn't realize how short the time was.

When she passed on November 25th, the lawyer contacted us, telling us that not only were we to execute her will, but also everything she owned had been left to us. We were stunned.

We didn't have a chance to ask her why she had made this decision. We were certainly baffled by it. She had a brother that she had raised as a son. Wouldn't he have wanted everything?

It turns out that because they were estranged, she chose us instead. She had a sister in Florida and several other distant family members. As we went through all her possessions in her home (which she also left for us), we found many things that we were sure the family would want.

There were requests from family members for certain items, which we gladly gave them, letting them know to request whatever they wanted. Although there were a few requests, most items were sorted and sold at an estate sale. We do still have a few items, and I think of Myra every time I see these items.

The family was a little strange at the funeral when they realized that Jeff and I had been given everything. I totally understand that, and the situation made us feel very awkward. We had not asked for any of what we had been given, but I'm sure there was resentment. However, what was done was done.

Proverbs 22:28 tells us, "Do not move an ancient boundary stone set up by your ancestors."

When I read this verse, the previous story came to mind. God has given us an inheritance, both spiritually and physically. He gave us a spiritual inheritance through Jesus's death, burial and resurrection. But He also knows that when we move to Heaven someone will inherit our possessions, our legacy and possibly our mantle. Someone will inherit our "boundaries".

For some reason, God had decided we would inherit Myra's legacy. To bring a little context, I do believe God put it on Myra's heart in response to a word He spoke to Jeff a few years prior. God was using the relationship I had with Myra, along with the resources He had blessed her with to fulfill His word to us.

I don't remember the year, but Jeff came home from his job at an auto dealership one day telling me that God had told him we needed to pay off all debt within five years. Once we had direction from the Lord, we went to work to obey that word.

Jeff was great at his job, making very good money. We used every bonus he brought home to make a direct payment on the principle of our home. With the money left us from the sale of Myra's home and her retirement account, our debts were wiped clean.

We were in awe. Not only did God speak a word to us, but I also believe He saw our hearts and that we were willing to work to obey Him, so He dumped blessing on us to help fulfill that word.

In May 2000 we discovered the reason God needed us out of debt. God asked Jeff to quit his job in the car business and to begin working in the field of residential construction. Myra's house was the first we remodeled and sold.

Thank you to Myra Fuller for hearing God's voice and being part of His plan for our lives. And thank you Father in Heaven for guarding and fulfilling Your Word.

What has God spoken to you? What has He asked you to do? I recommend that you quickly do the next thing that looks like obedience, then keep being obedient. God may just show up to fulfill His word to you!

215

Day 253

I Am Not Afraid

Isaiah 6-7 / 2 Corinthians 11:16-33 / Psalm 54 / Proverbs 23:1-3

I love loud thunderstorms. I love the sights, the sounds, and that intense rumble that shakes the inside of my soul as the thunder reverberates through the atmosphere. I have several thunderstorm stories. I'm not sure why I'm not afraid of storms because one childhood event should have been enough to make me fearful. Maybe it is the grace of God I'm not afraid.

When I was about 10 years old, my sister and I attended a Girl Scout horseback riding camp. We were so excited! That was so many years ago that I don't remember much about the camp. I do remember they had oatmeal for breakfast – yuck! I also remember the day we were out with the horses, and a thunderstorm was heard in the distance.

I can't remember what we did with the horses, but we made our way into the tack house to wait for the storm to pass. The room was filled with little girls huddled together and waiting for the storm to end. My sister and I were leaning up against a Coke machine. The next thing we heard was a loud "crack" and then I remember being thrown across the room and blacking out for a few seconds.

The camp nurse said both my sister and I had entrance and exit burns from the electricity that had passed through our bodies. Lightning had struck the tree outside, gone through the underground wiring, up through the Coke machine and into our little girl bodies. We were so sick that night.

We were moved into the counselors' cabin so they could watch us, making sure we were okay. That night for dinner we had a new treat, no-bake cookies. Susan and I got to taste the cookies before dinner since we were in a room connected to the mess hall. That was one bright moment after our horrifying experience.

When I read Isaiah 6:1-4 about the seraphim with six wings flying above the throne and that at the sounds of their voices the doorposts and thresholds shook and the temple was filled with smoke, I can imagine the rumbling that was created. I'm sure that scene is much more intense and terrifying than a thunderstorm, but I also have a feeling I know a little of what it would have been like to be in the throne room of Heaven.

The doorposts and thresholds were shaking... there was a rumbling... and I can imagine the thunder that would make me smile and giggle at the sound. I am not afraid. Would I be in awe to see this Heavenly sight? Yes, I know I would be. But I also wonder if it would be familiar to me.

One year on vacation at the beach in Florida, I sat outside during a thunderstorm just so I could watch the dark clouds, see the lighting, and feel the thunder. One thunderclap was so loud that I jumped and screamed, and then I giggled.

The power that is contained in a storm is nothing compared to the power that is within and surrounding our Mighty God. Yet, I am also not afraid of Him. His love is powerful, yet kind. I feel safe with the power of who God is. I feel protected, watched over.

I feel that similar powerful rumble during a large worship gathering when the sound of the bass guitar is reverberating throughout the building. There is something about those low musical sounds that are very comforting to me. I wonder if Heaven will be a little like that. I wonder if I will be in awe of the greatness of God. I'm sure I will be. But I will not be afraid.

I have felt a small portion of His power, and it is not a fearful thing to me. His power is comforting. His power is that of a protective Father. That of one who sees His loved one being harmed and comes quickly to the rescue. I am not afraid.

Day 254

You Are a Heavenly Being

Isaiah 8-9 / 2 Corinthians 12:1-10 / Psalm 55 / Proverbs 23:4-5

Time travel and inter-dimensional travel are topics explored in science fiction novels and movies. However, have you ever considered that these two things may be real? Now, before you stop reading, thinking I'm crazy, allow me to prove to you that fact and fiction may have a relative thread. I know it seems far-fetched, but let's see what the scriptures say about these types of things.

2 Corinthians 12:2-4 tells us this:

"I was caught up to the third Heaven fourteen years ago. Whether I was in my body or out of my body, I don't know—only God knows. Yes, only God knows whether I was in my body or outside my body. But I do know that I was caught up to paradise and heard things so astounding that they cannot be expressed in words, things no human is allowed to tell."

Do you still think I'm crazy? If you believe that the Bible is true, and is the Holy Spirit inspired Word of God, then the account above is your first piece of proof of time and inter-dimensional travel. There are other examples in scripture, and I'll include those for you in a minute.

I am a huge science fiction fan. Before I began considering that these concepts may have a basis in fact, I said that I believed my love of science fiction was because the things of Heaven were probably more fantastic and unimaginable than anything we've ever considered. There is something about the genre of science fiction that fascinates me and causes me to believe that there is much more to discover in other realms than our minds can conceive.

Have I ever traveled through time? No. Have I ever been to Heaven? No. But I would certainly love to do both! I have a friend who has traveled through time as he traveled to another state. What should have been a multi-hour trip took just a couple of hours. He had no certain awareness that he had traveled through time, but he just knew that his trip was miraculously much shorter.

One of my daughters has also traveled into the future where she saw her younger sister and part of who she will become. Yes, I believe her. Yes, I'm excited about what she saw!

Are you ready for more proof?

"Enoch lived 365 years,
walking in close fellowship with God.
Then one day he disappeared,
because God took him."— Genesis 5:23-24

"It was by faith that Enoch was taken up to Heaven
without dying— 'he disappeared, because God took him.'
For before he was taken up, he was known
as a person who pleased God."—Hebrews 11:5

"When they came up out of the water,
the Spirit of the Lord snatched Philip away.
The eunuch never saw him again
but went on his way rejoicing."
—Acts 8:39

"It was the Lord's Day, and I was worshiping in the Spirit. Suddenly, I heard behind me a loud voice like a trumpet blast. It said, 'Write in a book everything you see, and send it to the seven churches in the cities of Ephesus, Smyrna, Pergamum, Thyatira, Sardis, Philadelphia, and Laodicea.'"— Revelation 1:10-11

You would need to read the entire book of Revelation to understand all that John described of what he saw and experienced. There was an interaction between John in the earthly realm and the things of Heaven in another realm. Whether John traveled to Heaven or just saw into Heaven I don't know, but there was a definite connection between the two realms.

Feel free to do more research and to ask God His thoughts on this topic. I believe we are seeing these interactions because God wants us to know we are Heavenly beings having an earthly experience. We have access to the Spirit realm through the indwelling of Holy Spirit in us. We have an inheritance in the supernatural and we are meant to bring that supernatural, Heavenly experience into earth.

Day 255

The 7 Spirits of God upon Jesus

Isaiah 10-11 / 2 Corinthians 12:11-21 / Psalm 56 / Proverbs 23:6-8

A few years ago, two friends and I studied and presented a video series called "The 7 Spirits of God." We took our inspiration from Isaiah 11:2, which is part of our reading today. I want to give you a little more information from The Passion Translation because it gives such great insight. (Note: all scripture and defining notes in this entry will be from TPT.)

I've heard that The Passion Translation of the Bible is one of the more accurate renditions from both the original Hebrew and Greek, as well as Aramaic. As one who appreciates accurate doctrine, I'm thankful to have found this translation from which to study.

After we reread the two verses, I want to give you a little more information on the 7 Spirits. I encourage you to do further study because there is not enough space or time for me to share the details of each one.

Isaiah 11:1-2, "The cut-off stump of Jesse will sprout, and a fruitful Branch will grow from his roots: the Spirit of Yahweh will rest upon him, the Spirit of Extraordinary Wisdom, the Spirit of Perfect Understanding, the Spirit of Wise Strategy, the Spirit of Mighty Power, the Spirit of Revelation, and the Spirit of the Fear of Yahweh."

Jesse being mentioned refers to the royal family line of King David, out of which came Jesus Christ. This prophecy is referring to Jesus while telling us about the Spirits of the Heavenly realm that will rest upon Him as He lives His sinless life on earth.

The first Spirit upon Jesus was the Spirit of Yahweh, which is defined as "the Spirit of prophecy, or the manifest presence of God," His Father. John 1:32-34 confirms this Spirit of Yahweh upon Jesus.

As John baptized Jesus, he proclaimed these words, "I see the Spirit of God appear like a dove descending from the Heavenly realm and landing upon him—and it remained on him! Before this I didn't know who he was. But the one who sent me to baptize with water had told me, 'You will see the Spirit come down and stay on someone. He will be the One I have sent to baptize with the Holy Spirit.' Now I have seen this happen and I can tell you for sure that this man is the Son of God.'"

The second Spirit that rested upon Jesus was the Spirit of Extraordinary Wisdom which is defined as "the Spirit of Skillfulness" (See Exodus 31:2-4). "This Spirit gives equipping ability for music, art, business, writing, creativity, and wisdom for judicial decisions."

The third Spirit upon Jesus was the Spirit of Perfect Understanding which is defined as "the Spirit of Intelligent Insight." "This Spirit imparts the ability to discern the truth, to know the meaning of riddles, and to decipher parables and allegories."

The fourth Spirit upon Jesus was the Spirit of Wise Strategy which is defined as "the Spirit of Guidance." "This is the Hebrew word *etsah* and is used numerous times in the Old Testament for 'counsel', 'advice', or 'purpose.' It is also used for steering (guiding) a ship. This anointing imparts the wisdom and counsel needed for spiritual leadership."

The fifth Spirit upon Jesus was the Spirit of Mighty Power which is defined as "the Spirit of a Mighty Warrior."

The sixth Spirit upon Jesus was the Spirit of Revelation which is defined as "the Spirit of Knowledge." "This is not knowledge that is learned from books or study but knowledge that comes from experiencing intimacy with God."

The seventh and final Spirit upon Jesus was the Spirit of the Fear of Yahweh which is defined as "a reverence and partnership with His Father."

The seven Spirits that were upon Jesus also rest upon His people. I encourage you to read the entry again, looking for clues of God's Spirit at work in your life.

Day 256

An Amazing Story

Isaiah 12-14 / 2 Corinthians 13:1-13 / Psalm 57 / Proverbs 23:9-11

"With joy you will drink deeply
from the fountain of salvation."—Isaiah 12:3

"Christ is not weak when He deals with you;
He is powerful among you."—2 Corinthians 13:3b

"He will send help from Heaven to rescue me,
disgracing those who hound me. My God will send forth His
unfailing love and faithfulness."—Psalm 57:3

I don't usually begin these daily entries with the scriptures that caught my eye, but something interesting happened today as I read. I noticed a pattern. The verses from both Isaiah and the Psalm were the third verse, so I decided to look at the third verse in 2 Corinthians and just as I suspected, they all three relate to one another. Three sets of three. Interesting. I wonder what God is saying.

I was first drawn to the joy experienced when we drink from the fountain of salvation. Then I was struck by God's love and faithfulness. Finally, I was reminded that He is powerful toward His people. Salvation is our deliverance from and victory over sin. It is God the Father through Jesus Christ the Son who accomplished this deliverance for us.

John 3:16 tells us why the Father sent the Son. "For God so loved the world that He gave His one and only Son." The Father sent the Son because of His great love.

It was the power of God that raised Jesus Christ from the dead and now raises us up with Him. The same power that raised Jesus Christ from the dead also lives in us and gives life to our bodies (See Romans 8:11).

Are you seeing the same story built from these three verses that I am? The story I saw is a rescue story. It is a story of salvation, love, and power. We are the objects of affection in the greatest of all love stories. Our hero is God who gave all He had to remove us from death and from the power of the evil one.

Once we are aware that salvation has been freely offered, we are invited to come and draw water from that fountain. Did you know salvation is offered from fountains? Most fountains provide an endless supply of water. The wells of salvation are certainly wells that do not run dry.

I'm reminded of a song we've sung many times.

"There is a fountain filled with blood, drawn from Emmanuel's veins. And sinners plunged beneath that flood, lose all their guilty stains."

Floods also indicate an endless supply. And since we are speaking about what Jesus provided on the cross through the willing gift of His life, we know that we have endless grace, forgiveness, love, mercy, and any other thing we have need of. We are invited to draw from God knowing that His supply will never run out.

Whatever it is that we need, He has it in abundance. He doesn't grow tired or weary of our asking or of His giving. He gives and gives without the level of His reservoir ever lowering.

What are you in need of today? What does it seem you are missing from your experience, whether you are a follower of Christ or not? I invite you to ask God to meet your need. He will meet you with His salvation, His power, and His love.

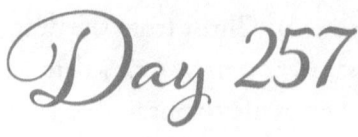

Day 257

The Message of Truth

Isaiah 15-18 / Galatians 1 / Psalm 58 / Proverbs 23:12

Truth is said by some to be relative. Relative to what? Isn't truth, truth? Some would say that truth varies based upon the situation. I don't call that truth; I call that the creative solution to a certain problem in a moment.

There is one body of truth that I believe is foundational to all of life. If we attempt to make a foundation of then build upon any other body of beliefs, we will find our houses falling for lack of stability.

Galatians 1:9 is very direct when it states: "As we have already said, so now I say again: If anybody is preaching to you a gospel other than what you accepted, let them be under God's curse!"

Let's define two words before we explore how scary that statement is. The word for "gospel" is defined as "good news." The word for "curse" is defined as "a person or thing doomed to destruction."

Y'all, this sounds like bad news to me! Reading that verse causes me to want to get the message of the gospel correct so that I remain under God's blessing and not His curse. Of course, since I'm His, I do not believe I can be under His curse. Holy Spirit is working in and through us to reveal His truth, and for that we must be thankful.

This verse is likely referring to those who claim to know Jesus Christ but do not actually know Him. Perhaps this message is spoken to those who would use a false message to gain followers for financial gain or to make themselves feel important. Unbelievably, this happens. I have a hard time understanding people who would intentionally deceive others, but sadly they exist.

If you hear a message, how do you know you're hearing the truth? Holy Spirit will witness the message within your heart. In other words, through discernment you'll know whether what you're hearing is truth. You'll also be able to discern the motives of the one bringing the message.

The message of the gospel is simple, yet profound. Romans 1:16 in The Passion Translation reads, "I refuse to be ashamed of the wonderful message of God's liberating power unleashed in us through Christ! For I am thrilled to preach that everyone who believes is saved—the Jew first, and then people everywhere!"

The wonderful message mentioned in that verse is the gospel and it has the power to set people free from sin, sickness, and demonic influence. No other message can do that! Only the gospel can bring freedom to someone. Jesus paid for our freedom and as we share the message, Holy Spirit is present to cause people to believe the message and to receive His miracles. That is the message I want to believe and share.

Can you imagine sharing a message that is said to be good news, yet no one is changed by it? No one healed, no one delivered from demons, and no one who comes to know Christ. What a waste of time and energy! I have no interest in wasting my time preaching or listening to such powerless messages.

Lord, make us aware of Your truth. Lead us toward Your message in the earth, and away from all false messages. Give us discernment and give us the courage to combat all false messages.

Day 258

Laugh with God

Isaiah 19-21 / Galatians 2:1-16 / Psalm 59 / Proverbs 23:13-14

There are several verses in the Psalms where it says that God laughs at His enemies. He mocks them, He scorns them, and He is certainly not afraid of them. Of course, He would not be afraid because He is God who is all powerful. What about you and me? Have you ever laughed at an enemy?

Maybe you were instead shaking in your boots or hiding for fear they would physically hurt you. And maybe they did hurt you physically or emotionally. How do you suppose God felt about someone hurting you? I would say it made Him sad or even angry. Just as you would be upset when someone hurt someone you love, God is upset when His people are mistreated. But what do you suppose makes Him laugh?

> "But you laugh at them, LORD;
> you scoff at all those nations."—Psalm 59:8

I believe God laughs because He knows the end of the story. He knows that the enemy loses all things when everything is said and done. God will defend and protect us even when evil is attempting to destroy us. We may suffer and feel the pain of the attack, but we belong to Jesus Christ, and we do not need to fear.

God laughs because satan will be defeated and placed into a lake of fire for all eternity. He may cause pain and suffering now but his end is the worst possible scenario for a traitor. And we must live with that in mind. We must remember that we have authority over the enemy now and that his end is coming soon.

There have been times I laughed, both at the enemy and at those he is using to inflict pain upon my family and me. Maybe I laugh because I know neither has any power over me since I belong to Jesus Christ. Maybe I laugh because I am healed and strong. Maybe I laugh because I have the perspective of Heaven. I was not always able to laugh.

There was a time when I was angry, hurt, depressed and in tears. But I chose not to stay in that frame of mind. We have choices. We cannot choose what happens to us, but we can choose how we respond. Do I accept the evil plans, or reject them? Do I complain and whine about my suffering, or do I trust God to deliver me?

I have honestly done both. I have gotten better about keeping my eyes fixed on Jesus in the hard things, knowing I can't change what is happening apart from His intervention. And I know He wants to intervene. He wants to heal, deliver and set us free. He also wants to do that for those who are treating us as enemies.

Pray for those who persecute you. Forgive them and ask God to bless them. Why? Because then you will be healed and blessed. And maybe they will be also. We never know when God might use our prayers to heal and deliver our oppressors.

On a practical note, laughter is said to be like medicine. (See Proverbs 17:22) So, find something funny and have a good laugh. Or remember all God has done for you and allow joy to fill your soul.

Whatever you do, do not permit anger or bitterness to fill your soul; you will certainly regret that. Laugh at your enemies. Remember that God is also laughing, and I have a feeling that when He laughs all of Heaven shakes.

Day 259

Let God Arise, Goodbye Enemies!

Isaiah 22-24 / Galatians 2:17-3:9 / Psalm 60 / Proverbs 23:15-16

I enjoy movies where the theme is that classic struggle between good and evil. In the movies, good always wins. And guess what? The same is true of real life. It may appear as if evil has the upper hand, but things are not as they appear on the surface. Jesus Christ has already won the entire war. We may have battles and skirmishes, and we may suffer loss, but in the end, we win! If victory depended only on you and me, all would be lost. However, since we are in Christ, victory is ours.

> "Yet even in the midst of all these things,
> we triumph over them all, for God has made us to be
> more than conquerors, and His demonstrated love is
> our glorious victory over everything!"—Romans 8:37

I also love this verse from Psalm 68:1, "God! Arise with awesome power, and every one of your enemies will scatter in fear!"

I'm already feeling powerful! In our reading today I came across another amazing verse that follows this line of thinking.

> "With God we will gain the victory,
> and he will trample down our enemies."—Psalm 60:12

These three examples are only a tiny portion of all the kick butt, take names verses in the Bible. When Father God sent His Son Jesus

Christ to the earth, He sent Him to destroy the works of the enemy. Father loves destroying the enemies' works and plans. Jesus destroyed those works and plans while on earth and at the cross, and now it is our turn to do some damage.

Maybe you were taught that good boys and girls don't get angry or violent. But there is a time for both. When injustice is ruling, or the enemy is robbing from another human being, it is time to rise and fight in the power of the Spirit of God. Our warfare is not like that of the world. We don't use guns and knives; we use powerful Spirit weapons such as love and faith.

We have a sword called the Word of God. When the enemy comes against you with lies and violence, find some verses that will remind him of the truth and of who you belong to. He has no power over you because all he can do is lie. If his lips are moving, you can be assured that what you're hearing is not true.

Is he accusing you? Is he minimizing who you are? All lies. You are a child of God. You are a son or daughter. You are kings and priests before your God. You have been knighted with, or delegated, the authority of Jesus Christ. He gained that authority for you on the cross when He made a joke of the devil, taking back the keys of death, hell and the grave. You have everything; the enemy has nothing.

All authority has been given to the Son by the Father and He is placing that same authority inside us. If Jesus Christ has all authority, the devil has none. The only way the devil can gain anything in our lives is if we choose to believe his lies. Nothing he tells us is truth, so we can ignore it all.

If you're having a day where you feel weak, call on God and ask Him to infuse you with His strength and power. Romans 6:10-11 in TPT says this,

"For by His sacrifice He died to sin's power once and for all, but He now lives continuously for the Father's pleasure. So let it be the same way with you! Since you are now joined with Him, you must continually view yourselves as dead and unresponsive to sin's appeal while living daily for God's pleasure in union with Jesus, the Anointed One."

Everything that Jesus has was transferred to us when we were born again. We are no longer that old person; we are completely new creations. Inside each one of us is the mighty power of God. This is the same power that was used to create the universe, including all of us. Through Jesus Christ, there is nothing we cannot accomplish.

Day 260

The Way to God's City

Isaiah 25:1-28:13 / Galatians 3:10-22 / Psalm 61 / Proverbs 23:17-18

As a musician and artist, I'm fascinated when a scripture is said to have been a song or poem. I've been aware of some songs in scripture but not every translation reveals this truth, so some songs may be hidden within the verses. I found such a song in Isaiah 26 today that may span several chapters. It was the notes in The Passion Translation that alerted me to this hidden song.

Isaiah 26:1-4, 12, "A day is coming when this song will be sung in the land of Judah: 'The city is a stronghold for us! The Lord's salvation, like inner and outer walls, makes it secure. Open the gates and let a righteous, faith-filled people enter in. Perfect, absolute peace surrounds those whose imaginations are consumed with you; they confidently trust in you. Yes, trust in the Lord Yahweh forever and ever! For Yah, the Lord God, is your Rock of Ages! Lord Yahweh, you will establish peace and prosperity for us, for all we have accomplished is the result of what you work through us.'"

The city spoken of here is the Kingdom of God, and even as I read the description of the inner and outer walls being made of the Lord's salvation, a picture began to form in my mind. The gates of salvation (just like the walls - I also assume the gates are made of salvation) open and allow the city to fill with people. There is no other way into God's Kingdom, except through Jesus Christ, our Salvation.

John 10:7-9, "I tell you the truth, I am the gate for the sheep. All who came before me were thieves and robbers. But the true sheep did not listen to them. Yes, I am the gate. Those who come in through me will be saved. They will come and go freely and will find good pastures."

Jesus is the gate by which people may enter the city, or Kingdom of God. There is no other way to enter. One may not go over the wall, or under, or around. One may only enter by the gate and that only if he or she has the permission of the gatekeeper. The "permission" required to enter is the blood of Jesus Christ.

Once you have entered the gate of Jesus Christ by permission of His blood shed on the cross, you have an opportunity. If you set your imagination (the things you think and dream about) on Him, absolute peace will surround and consume you. Just as there is no other way into God's city, there is no other way to obtain peace except through Jesus Christ.

Some believe peace is simple quiet; it is much more than that. The word "shalom" is defined as "wholeness, wellness, well-being, safe, happy, friendly, favor, completeness, to make peace, peace offering, secure, to prosper, to be victorious, to be content, tranquil, quiet, and restful."

So, the word Shalom is used to describe those of us who have been provided with all that is needed to be whole and complete and to break off all authority that would attempt to bind us to chaos.

I love that last part because in Shalom we have authority to forbid chaos into our lives and into the lives of those we love. Speak "Shalom" over yourself and those you love and as you do, remind yourself of all that word means. It's powerful!

Day 261

My Soul Finds Rest

Isaiah 28:14-30:11 / Galatians 3:23-4:31 / Psalm 62 / Proverbs 23:19-21

The craziness in this world is not stopping. The spiritual atmosphere has been thick, heavy, and sometimes depressive for a few years now. Many are becoming weary, tired, and tempted to give up the fight. But we must not do that.

The enemy is counting on our fatigue so that we will no longer stand in the Spirit. It is the Lord who gives us strength to continue to stand. There are times when the fight is exhausting and even standing seems like a huge task.

In those times be assured that the Lord is with you. His Spirit remains strong and steadfast even when you are in danger of losing hope. I believe all it takes is one glance in His direction or one whispered prayer and He is right there close by, ready to give you what you need. Our God does not grow tired, and He never loses hope. He is completely in charge, and He knows the end of the story.

Thankfully, I came across a refreshing couple of verses in today's scriptures.

Psalm 62:1-2 says this:

> "Truly my soul finds rest in God;
> my salvation comes from Him.
> Truly He is my rock and my salvation;
> He is my fortress; I will never be shaken."

I love the definition for the word "rest" in verse 1. The meaning of this word brings rest just reading it. It means "silence, still, repose, still waiting, quiet, ease from pain, the silent expectation of divine aid, confidence placed in God."

Add this meaning to that of the word "salvation" and one is beginning to feel a little hope returning. The Hebrew word for "salvation" in verse 1 is "yesua", pronounced yesh-oo-aw. Does that remind anyone else of the Hebrew name for Jesus? It does me! The meaning of this powerful word is "deliverance, prosperity, and victory." It also means "that which is delivered and safe."

One final word I want to highlight is the word "rock". The definition of this word, among other things, is "place of security, symbol of firmness, figurative of God as support and defense of His people."

I hope you are feeling stronger after reading these definitions. I know it's helping me. The craziness in the world may not subside any time soon and the oppressive spiritual atmosphere may continue for a time, but we have a safe place in God that we can run to. Honestly, we should remember that we are always hidden in Him, and not just during the difficult seasons.

I encourage you to hide in Him right now, read those verses above out loud, and sit in His presence. Your circumstances may not change right away, but you will have peace in your soul. May God bless and strengthen you today!

Day 262

A Treasure and A Key

Isaiah 30:12-33:9 / Galatians 5:1-12 / Psalm 63 / Proverbs 23:22

Yesterday we talked about rest for our souls. Today I found a rich treasure chest stuffed full of amazing things. Sometimes when we find a treasure chest, it is locked and there is no key. The treasure chest I found has a key and I'm excited to share it with you. I have a feeling this treasure is one that has no bottom and no limit. There is more than enough for all of us with plenty to spare.

> "The Lord is exalted, for he dwells on high;
> he will fill Zion with his justice and righteousness.
> He will be the sure foundation for your times, a rich store of
> salvation and wisdom and knowledge;
> the fear of the Lord is the key to this treasure."
> —Isaiah 33:5-6 (NIV)

Did you see the treasure chest in those verses? And did you see the key? How many of you have ever been fascinated by hidden or buried treasure? Probably all of you. The thought of gold, silver and precious jewels makes anyone's heart race.

Have you ever watched a movie or documentary where the diver dives down to the sunken ship, and as he nears the bottom you hold your breath waiting to see what he'll find? He gets to the bottom of the ocean floor, finds the chest, but can't open it because there is no key. Sure, the chest can be hauled up and broken open but it's so much better to have access to the key.

That's why this verse, which holds a treasure that won't rust or decay, is so intriguing. Imagine finding a chest filled with eternal treasure that you can "take with you" when you leave earth.

We're all aware that neither money nor possessions can go with us when we leave earth. Remembering this causes me to think about the Egyptians who created huge underground tombs where they were buried with all their earthly treasures. They were convinced that when they left this earth, they would be able to take all of that with them down the Nile River on Ra's magical boat. Sadly, for them, as those tombs were opened in modern times, all the treasure remained intact. None of it made it to the afterlife.

The Heavenly treasure though is different. This treasure chest in the verses above contains salvation, wisdom, and knowledge, not to mention that the Lord carries with Him both justice and righteousness. There are five treasures available for you and me, and we have the key! The key is the fear of the Lord.

We've talked about the fear of the Lord before. It's not the kind of fear where you are terrified of someone. This fear is reverence and awe. It's a fear that causes us to want to please and obey our Heavenly Father. When we fear the Lord in this way, we will have access to all five components of this treasure. And we can possess this treasure in an unlimited supply.

We have salvation, wisdom, knowledge, justice, and righteousness and that's just for starters. We've talked several times about the riches found in Christ that belong to those of us who are daughters and sons. Since we already own all these treasures, all we need to do is hold out our hands, ask God to use what is ours, and thank Him for the gifts.

I pray today that you will know the riches that He has purchased for you. The purchase price was the blood of Jesus Christ. Yes, it was a steep price to pay, but we are, after all, speaking of eternal treasure.

Day 263

The Highway of Holiness

Isaiah 33:10-36:22 / Galatians 5:13-26 / Psalm 64 / Proverbs 23:23

Have any of you ever been afraid of scary monsters under the bed? I'll admit I used to be afraid of the dark and monsters. Yes, I know they aren't real, but there are still times I hate looking under the bed!

We know that all we'll find are some dust bunnies and maybe a forgotten pair of shoes. That said, I'm reminded that not all dangers are those we can see. There are spiritual dangers all around, and the enemy is waiting to set a trap for us to fall into.

I believe that if we'll listen, God will warn us of potential traps. Sometimes that trap looks like a sin that we willfully walk into instead of running the other way as we should. The enemy knows our weak areas, and he knows how to push our buttons.

He's been working on these evil plans for years and he has developed a certain level of skill in terrorizing men, women, and children. There is no need to fear or get discouraged though. There are safe places for us to walk both in the natural and in the Spirit realm.

Isaiah 35:8-10 talks about a safe path.

"And a highway will be there; it will be called the Way of Holiness; it will be for those who walk on that Way. The unclean will not journey on it; wicked fools will not go about on it. No lion will be found there, nor any ravenous beast; they will not be found there. But only the redeemed will walk there, and those the LORD has rescued will return. They will enter Zion with singing; everlasting joy will crown their heads. Gladness and joy will overtake them, and sorrow and sighing will flee away."

How does one find this safe highway? It sounds like a wonderful road to travel on. The Way of Holiness is available only to those who step onto the highway through Jesus Christ. For everyone else, the entrance is hidden.

Once we've begun walking on this highway, we can rest assured that only those who are part of our new family in God will be walking along with us. There may be impostors who will try to invade, but with discernment they will quickly be discovered and removed.

It's interesting that this scripture says no lions will be found there. I can think of one such lion that I would be glad to never see again! How can the verse say he will not be there?

Does this mean the devil cannot derail or stop us? Or that he cannot remove us from the highway? Because of what Jesus accomplished on the cross, he has no teeth and no power. However, we must remember that he does gain power over us when we agree with him. Therefore, we must always disagree with his plan and lies!

When we read about Zion, this refers to our final destination, the end of our journey. Those on earth might call that death, but those of us who are in Christ understand that our final destination is not death but eternal life. We will enter our eternal reward and be introduced to our new home. There will be great joy and singing. Can you imagine!

Even if our journey on earth has been hard, and all our lives have difficulty, the end of the journey will be the greatest rejoicing we've ever experienced. Our tears and sorrow will be gone. I don't believe we will even remember the difficult times we walked through on earth because we will be face-to-face with the One who snatched us away from the hands of evil and death.

Here is another passage that refers to another highway, the highway to hell.

Matthew 7:13-14, "You can enter God's Kingdom only through the narrow gate. The highway to hell is broad, and its gate is wide for the many who choose that way. But the gateway to life is very narrow and the road is difficult, and only a few ever find it."

The Way of Holiness and the highway to hell. Two paths. Two gates or entrances. Two experiences and two destinations. And everyone is free to choose which path they will walk on. These are sobering thoughts, and a sobering choice faces each one of us. May we hear His voice and may we say, "Yes" to His offer of eternal life.

"For, 'everyone who calls on the name
of the LORD will be saved.'"—Romans 10:13

Romans 10:9, "If you openly declare that Jesus is Lord and believe in your heart that God raised him from the dead, you will be saved. For it is by believing in your heart that you are made right with God, and it is by openly declaring your faith that you are saved."

Day 264

We Are Blessed to Be a Blessing

Isaiah 37-38 / Galatians 6 / Psalm 65 / Proverbs 23:24

Sharing our belongings with others is one of our first lessons as little children. Little ones do not always understand the necessity of sharing because everything that comes into their hands is in their eyes "mine". Hitting, biting, crying, and screaming are all typical responses when one does not want to share. While it seems normal for children to act this way, once we become adults, these behaviors are frowned upon.

Can you imagine coming upon a group of adults who are reluctant to share their "toys" – their cars, houses, boats, etc. - so they are hitting one another and crying? Picturing that scene makes me laugh! While adults don't outwardly show their reluctance to share, they may seethe inwardly at the thought of either sharing or giving away what they have. Stingy adults are poor adults.

Why do I say that? If sowing and reaping is true – it is a law God set into place – then when we share and give, we are sowing into a spiritual system that will grow blessings for us and our family. We don't give to get, but we do give from the heart to be a blessing. As we do that, I believe God piles blessings up on our account and we will see those pour out in various ways.

One way we can sow into God's Kingdom is by sharing what we have with those who teach us. Galatians 6:6-10 in The Passion Translation is instructive on this topic.

"And those who are taught the Word must share all good things with their teacher. God will never be mocked! For what you plant will always be the very thing you harvest. The harvest you reap reveals the seed that you planted. If you plant the corrupt seeds of self-life into this natural realm, you can expect a harvest of corruption. If you plant the good seeds of Spirit-life you will reap beautiful fruits that grow from the everlasting life of the Spirit. And don't allow yourselves to be weary in planting good seeds, for the season of reaping the wonderful harvest you've planted is coming! Take advantage of every opportunity to be a blessing to others, especially to our brothers and sisters in the family of faith!"

I don't want to dive into the topic of tithing right now, but that is one aspect of sharing with those who teach or instruct you in the Word of God. There are other ways to be a blessing. I think that when we seek to share with others apart from our regular tithe, being led by Holy Spirit is both wise and exciting. Why would that be exciting?

Because everything we do should be done with grace and a heart of love, led by our relationship with Jesus Christ. If all aspects of our walk with Jesus are filtered through these three – grace, love, and relationship – we will do well in life and God will be pleased. He isn't looking to make sure we follow certain rules; He wants us to be a blessing to others because that is how He created us.

He blessed us so that we could be a blessing to others. He didn't bless us to make us "fat" and "full". He gives an abundance so we will share. God is a giving, sharing, and loving Being and since we are created in His image, it makes sense that we would be the same.

Who teaches you the Word or supports you spiritually? How can you be a blessing to that person today? Ask God to show you and He will speak. I'm sure of it!

Beyond that, who else can you bless? If not with resources, perhaps you can bless someone with words of encouragement or a small act of kindness. All of these go a long way toward being a blessing to our brothers and sisters in the faith.

Day 265

A Secret Plan Revealed

Isaiah 39:1-41:16 / Ephesians 1 / Psalm 66 / Proverbs 23:25-28

I have mentioned this before, but I'll say it again. I love a good mystery! I love knowing there is a mystery. I love looking at the clues and trying to figure out the facts, and I enjoy learning the solution that may not be obvious to everyone. I am by no means Sherlock Holmes; I don't know that I could be a criminal investigator as I'm too sensitive to pain and suffering.

Once I discovered there were many mysteries hidden in the Bible, and many mysteries hidden in Jesus Christ, I knew I would never grow tired of reading, discovering clues and gaining relational knowledge about God. Consider this. God is nothing like us. Not only is He powerful, but He also loves us deeply. This is a conundrum that we must investigate! The God who created all things loves us. Unfathomable.

The book of Ephesians is one of those mysterious books. We hear about such topics as predestination, adoption, the mystery of His will, and that we are marked in God with a seal.

I don't see how I'll cover just one of these mysteries in this post, however, I'll do my best to choose only one. Perhaps you can read about the others, or perhaps I need to do an in-depth study of this book of the Bible at a future date.

Please read Ephesians 1:9-10, 13, 17-18 from The Passion Translation because there are several fascinating topics included in these verses, the whole chapter really! I'll choose one fascinating topic to dive deeper into, leaving the others for you to explore.

Here are verses 9-10: "And through the revelation of the Anointed One, he unveiled his secret desires to us—the hidden mystery of his long-range plan, which he was delighted to implement from the very beginning of time. And because of God's unfailing purpose, this detailed plan will reign supreme through every period of time until the fulfillment of all the ages finally reaches its climax—when God makes all things new in all of Heaven and earth through Jesus Christ."

It was difficult to choose which topic to explore, but I chose the hidden mystery of His long-range plan or will. God doesn't have a plan just for your life while you're on earth, although that is part of it. He has a plan that spans many generations, centuries, and people from all over the world.

Do you remember the story of Adam and Eve who were deceived by the serpent? Prior to this deception, Adam and Eve met with God in the garden daily to talk and spend time together. They had an unbroken fellowship. Once the serpent deceived them, Adam and Eve were separated from God by sin. In one moment, their fellowship with God and the authority He had given them to rule the earth was lost.

Man's fellowship with God and his authority to rule the earth were taken away that day. However, God was not taken by surprise. God knew because of His omniscient (all-knowing) nature that the devil was going to disrupt the beauty that had been created.

Satan couldn't stand the thought of God having something beautiful, so he sought immediately to destroy it. What the enemy didn't know was that God had already formed a plan to redeem or buy back what had been lost – a plan that He will see through until the end!

Men, women, and children would have to wait for many centuries for this plan to be enacted. However, the day finally came when a baby was born on earth whose mother agreed for the Holy Spirit to impregnate her. Does that sound scandalous? I'm sure it does. But there was no other way. Jesus had to come as a man to buy back those the Father created and loved.

When Jesus took His final breath on the cross, and went into hell to demolish the devil's kingdom, the secret plan was finally understood by the one who had attempted to destroy it all. In that moment, satan knew he had lost, and that God had accomplished the great feat of restoring to His created ones the fellowship and authority that had been stolen.

Yes, we must access these stolen things through a relationship with Jesus Christ. But our access to the Father has been restored. We once again possess all the powerful, beautiful things that are hidden in Christ Jesus.

How do we access what was lost? We say, "Yes" to the gift of Jesus Christ on the cross. We believe in our hearts and confess with our mouths that Jesus Christ is Lord, and we are saved!

Day 266

Speak Peace in the Earth

Isaiah 41:17-43:13 / Ephesians 2 / Psalm 67 / Proverbs 23:29-35

Leave me in peace. I just need some peace and quiet. The peace of God. May she rest in peace. A peace that passes understanding. Perfect peace. World peace. Peace of mind.

Have you ever taken time to study the word peace and find out what it really means? We may think it means quiet or the absence of chaos in our lives, and that is true. Did you know there are different words for "peace" in scripture?

I've written previously about the word Shalom. Today I want to explore a different word for peace: Eirene, pronounced i-ray-nay.

Ephesians 2:14-17 in The Passion Translation, "Our reconciling 'Peace' is Jesus! He has made Jew and non-Jew one in Christ. By dying as our sacrifice, he has broken down every wall of prejudice that separated us and has now made us equal through our union with Christ. Ethnic hatred has been dissolved by the crucifixion of his precious body on the cross. The legal code that stood condemning every one of us has now been repealed by his command. His triune essence has made peace between us by starting over—forming one new race of humanity, Jews and non-Jews fused together in himself! Two have now become one, and we live restored to God and reconciled in the body of Christ. Through his crucifixion, hatred died. For the Messiah has come to preach this sweet message of peace to you, the ones who were distant, and to those who are near."

Let's begin with a definition of the word "Eirene."

It means, "a state of national tranquility, (we could certainly use some of that!) exemption from the rage and havoc of war, (yep, need that!) peace between individuals, security, safety, prosperity, and salvation."

Reading these definitions reminds me of another scripture from Romans 5:1, also in The Passion Translation.

"Our faith in Jesus transfers God's righteousness to us and he now declares us flawless in his eyes. This means we can now enjoy true and lasting peace with God, all because of what our Lord Jesus, the Anointed One, has done for us."

Jesus is our only source for true peace. Those around us are currently crying out for and wishing we all had peace in the earth, but apart from God's Spirit being allowed to rule, we will not have lasting peace. That first definition of "national tranquility" is interesting because some people think that peace is only within our inner selves. This definition proves that God can bring peace into a nation.

How do you suppose God brings peace into a nation? Does He just speak and a blanket of quiet settles over everyone? Or does he put peace in the water, and we drink it? No, it is the job of the Church to be Christ in the earth.

We are the peace in the earth because we carry the Spirit of God. We are love, joy, patience, kindness, the glory of God, and many other beautiful things.

It's time for the Church to understand both her identity and her role in the earth. It is vital that we get this. We are the representation of Christ in the earth. We are the peace and presence of God. Where we go, when we are operating under the control of God's Spirit, we are bringing His solution to the world. And right now, the world needs what we have!

This is not a time to shrink back and be timid, or to forget who we are and become lazy. The world needs what we carry. They need our strength and courage, our confidence and yes, our peace. While the rest of the world cowers in fear, the Church is meant to arise in boldness with a deep inner knowledge of who she was created to be.

Will you answer this call? Will you investigate God's Word and hear from His heart, reminding yourself of who you are so you can shine in the earth? You are needed, mighty warrior. There are many around you who are fearful and unsure about what is happening. But no matter what is happening, we have the answer to every question, and His name is Jesus. Offer this answer today to those who are fearful, giving them courage.

Day 267

The Voice of a Woman

Isaiah 43:14-45:10 / Ephesians 3 / Psalm 68:1-18 / Proverbs 24:1-2

The voices of God's people have been silenced throughout all of history. Some allowed themselves to be silenced, and some rose to speak regardless of the consequences. There has been a trend in the earth that the voices of women ought to be silenced, quieted, and subjected to authoritarian rule by those who believe women are not equal in value to men. Before I go further, this will not be a "man bashing" entry. I don't abide by such behavior.

All voices are equal in value according to the Father and the Son, Jesus Christ. As a matter of fact, when one reads the Gospels (Matthew, Mark, Luke and John) it is obvious that Jesus treated women as equals. Yes, the roles are different because regardless of gender, we are each equipped and suited toward different callings. Men are stronger physically, although watching a woman give birth makes me wonder how strength is measured.

Most women are more nurturing and are therefore the ones who take the main role in raising children. Both genders are gifted to work inside or outside the home. Why am I speaking about this? While reading Psalm 68 today, I found an interesting verse in The New Living Translation.

Verse 11 says, "The Lord announces the word, and the women who proclaim it are a mighty throng."

This Psalm is about victory over the enemies of God's people.

Verse one begins with, "May God arise, may His enemies be scattered; may His foes flee before Him." I believe it is a good day for God to arise! When we arise, not much may happen because we are not that scary. But when Holy Spirit is within us and we arise, world watch out! When God arises... It's over!

As God's enemies are being scattered, the Lord is announcing victory, and the women are telling the story of victory through God. That sounds like some women preachers to me!

Typically, the men went into battle, coming home with stories of victory to tell their families. I'm sure the women enjoyed repeating these stories among the community as the men recovered from war. Remember also that many of the stories from scripture began as oral stories. Someone did eventually write them down, thankfully. I'm glad we have the stories and histories to read today.

What about these women being trusted with the message of victory? How did Jesus treat women? They traveled with Him, supported Him and were part of His team.

It was the women who discovered the empty tomb and went to tell the other followers of Jesus what had happened. It was a Samaritan woman who Jesus met at the well, telling her all about her life. What did she do? She went into her village and told everyone about what Jesus had done, making her the first woman evangelist.

Women's voices have value. Women have a message to share that God has put within them. Blessed is the man who is secure enough in his calling to support and push forward the women in his life.

I am blessed to have a man like that. He knows who he is in Christ and is therefore able to cheer me on as I pursue who God has called me to be. What about you? Are you using your voice to further God's Kingdom? Are you pushing past the resistance? I encourage you to open your mouth and let God fill it with His message!

Day 268

Is God a Wooden Statue?

Isaiah 45:11-48 / Ephesians 4:1-16 / Psalm 68:19-35 / Proverbs 24:3-4

As I've read in Isaiah the last few days, I've been curious as to why anyone would worship something that was created. Isn't the one who made the thing greater than the created thing? Many verses speak about idols made from wood or metal.

How can an object made of wood or metal hear your prayers? Or answer and give you any kind of power? It's not logical that praying to a statue would be of any benefit, yet people still do it. I suppose that's what it looks like when one is deceived.

There is a lot of deception on the earth; there always has been since the incident in the garden when the serpent attacked and deceived Eve. We all have areas where we remain deceived. For those who have received Jesus Christ, full revelation of truth will not come until we are in Heaven. For now, we do our best to listen to God's Spirit to help us discern the truth.

Here is one verse that has me considering the deception of worshipping created objects. Isaiah 45:20, "Gather together and come; assemble you fugitives from the nations. Ignorant are those who carry about idols of wood, who pray to gods that cannot save."

Like I said, the past few chapters have been filled with verses just like this one. Those who worship idols of wood are called "ignorant". Those who are ignorant have no knowledge; they don't know any better. Either they haven't been taught, or they've been taught the wrong things, and no one has ever shown them the truth. Sometimes people don't believe it when you tell them the truth; they need a demonstration of some kind. The power of God can demonstrate and validate who He is.

Isaiah 45:24, 25 states who God really is. "They will say of me, 'in the LORD alone are deliverance and strength.' All who have raged against Him will come to Him and be put to shame. But all the descendants of Israel will find deliverance in the LORD and will make their boast in Him."

Isaiah 46:4 reveals to us how God truly cares for those who are His. "Even to your old age and gray hairs I am He, I am He who will sustain you. I have made you and I will carry you; I will sustain you and I will rescue you."

Why would one not want to look to this God for answers and help? There are those who don't believe God is real. What harm would it do to ask Him to reveal Himself? What have you got to lose?

I've said before that if I'm wrong in believing that God is real, I've lost nothing. If others are wrong in believing He doesn't exist, they have lost everything. We will all know the truth one day. I pray everyone knows on this side of eternity.

I have a challenge, and this challenge applies whether you believe God is real or not. Ask God to show you who He is. Speak out to "whomever" and then wait for an answer, either audible, or in your heart or seen with your eyes.

One never knows how the Creator may choose to reveal Himself. If there is a creation, there is a Creator. Even logic would tell us that much. I pray you find the Creator today because He also has the instruction manual for your life and for why He made you as He did.

Day 269

Weigh Your Words Carefully

Isaiah 48:12-50:11 / Ephesians 4:17-32 / Psalm 69:1-18 / Proverbs 24:5-6

When our children were small, we talked to them about the words they used and the attitudes they chose. Any time one of them had something unkind to say, Jeff would usually remind them of Ephesians 4:29. This verse is often used when someone says a "bad word", but this verse applies to more than just bad language.

Ephesians 4:29 in The Passion Translation reads:

> "And never let ugly or hateful words
> come from your mouth, but instead let your words
> become beautiful gifts that encourage others;
> do this by speaking words of grace to help them."

Have you seen the studies done where positive words were spoken over water molecules under a microscope and then negative words were spoken over the same water? When the positive words were spoken, the water molecules formed beautiful patterns. When the negative words were spoken the water "splatted" itself into a chaotic mess. If water reacts this way, how might humans react to the same treatment?

Did you know that we are made up biologically of 60% water overall. Our brain and heart are 73% water, and our lungs are 83% water. The skin is 64%, the muscles and kidneys are 79% and our bones are 31% water. I have a feeling that when kind words filled with life are spoken over us, we make a beautiful inward pattern. And when unkindness is spoken, our cells turn into splatters of chaos, potentially causing disease.

If words have damaged our DNA, how would we heal our bodies again? My first suggestion would be to forgive the one who spoke unkindly to us. I believe forgiveness heals our cells, our DNA, and our entire body and soul. When our souls are healthy, our bodies are healthy. Our souls are key to our overall health.

What about when we are the ones speaking negative words? The resonance of those harmful words must travel through the speaker's body, being heard by the speaker's ears. May I be so bold as to say that the one who speaks evil is condemning herself to disease? That's even more incentive to speak life over others!

If you are reading this and have become aware that your words have been harmful, may I encourage you to get in touch with that one you spoke to and ask forgiveness? I have had to do that many times. What about if you are speaking harmful words to yourself? It counts as well. We must also speak life over our own bodies and souls.

So, if a destructive thought is threatening to come out of your mouth, stop yourself, praying to ask God to forgive your thoughts. If you can keep the words from exiting your lips, you may just save yourself and someone you love from harm. And your heart will thank you as well. Your heart doesn't want to hear those harmful inner words either.

My best advice is to speak life, health, peace and love as often as you can. Look for "excuses" to speak well of someone, especially of yourself!

Day 270

No Fear Even in the Shaking

Isaiah 51-53 / Ephesians 5 / Psalm 69:19-36 / Proverbs 24:7

With everything that's happening in our world right now, I'm always looking for strength and courage in scripture. I must remind myself that even when God's people go through hard things, His mercy covers us. Evil and wickedness are under judgment, and God's people are affected by that, but we are also protected by Him. That doesn't mean we won't suffer, but it does mean He is present.

All the reading in Isaiah chapters 51-53 was both eye-opening and encouraging today. I especially appreciated the promises I found in Isaiah 51:1-3 so I wanted to look at those three verses a little more closely. Here they are for you to read:

"Listen to me, all who hope for deliverance—all who seek the Lord! Consider the rock from which you were cut, the quarry from which you were mined. Yes, think about Abraham, your ancestor, and Sarah, who gave birth to your nation. Abraham was only one man when I called him. But when I blessed him, he became a great nation. The Lord will comfort Israel again and have pity on her ruins. Her desert will blossom like Eden, her barren wilderness like the garden of the Lord. Joy and gladness will be found there."

I love the imagery of having been cut from a rock and mined from a quarry. I imagine that means we are strong and courageous, as well as precious and rare. I'm reminded of how God is referred to as our Rock of salvation, making Him a strong place to stand.

When I think about Abraham and Sarah, who were patriarchs who followed God, and were the originators of an entire nation of people, I realize that we as the people of God were chosen long ago and the promises that He has made to us will be fulfilled by Him.

The Lord will comfort His people, especially in challenging times. God never leaves us nor forsakes us. He is always there as a strength and help in our times of need. The promise that our desert places will bloom brings great hope!

Deserts are dry and barren, but not when God is involved. He brings water and refreshment into the desert places in our lives and into His church. Joy and gladness will be found in those times of refreshment with the Lord. And I believe these times happen while difficult trials are all around.

Several years ago, I had the strong sense that both judgment and mercy would come crashing together soon. I didn't know when, but I knew it was coming. I feel we are living in those days now. In His wrath, may He remember mercy (Habakkuk 3:2).

So, if you're looking around and are fearful and uncertain of the future, remember who is really in charge. The Lord is sitting on His throne in Heaven but is also very involved in the lives of His people. He sees everything that is happening, and He is attempting to make wrongs right again. His is a fight for truth and justice.

When you're fearful, run to Him and He will cover you with the shadow of His hand! (Isaiah 51:16)

Day 271

Where Do You Go When Tired?

Isaiah 54:1-57:14 / Ephesians 6 / Psalm 70 / Proverbs 24:8

When you are thirsty, what is your favorite drink? Some love a good coca cola. Some love iced tea, and some love water. I've heard that only water will truly quench thirst as we're made up of about 60% water overall (we talked about that yesterday). I've heard that the tannins in tea can be dehydrating so even though we may think we're doing well to drink tea, it's potentially having the opposite effect. And don't even get me started on the ills of sodas!

Jesus is always talking to His people, letting them know that He has everything they need. He even calls out to those who do not believe in and trust Him, knowing He has everything they are looking for – peace, safety, satisfaction, and any other thing they would ever need. Please read these verses from Isaiah 55 and then let's talk!

"Is anyone thirsty? Come and drink—even if you have no money! Come, take your choice of wine or milk—it's all free! Why spend your money on food that does not give you strength? Why pay for food that does you no good? Listen to me, and you will eat what is good. You will enjoy the finest food. Come to me with your ears wide open. Listen, and you will find life. I will make an everlasting covenant with you. I will give you all the unfailing love I promised to David. See how I used him to display my power among the peoples. I made him a leader among the nations. You also will command nations you do not know, and peoples unknown to you will come running to obey, because I, the Lord your God, the Holy One of Israel, have made you glorious."— Isaiah 55:1-5

God is offering free food and drinks! Of course, these are not the food and drinks we think of when we're physically hungry or thirsty; these provisions will satisfy our souls. Have you ever felt a deep inner longing that you had no way to satisfy? Something felt off, or you felt empty, but you had no way to relieve the pain of that feeling. God's Spirit can fill that place.

Have you ever had an agitation in your soul that no matter what you did to fix it, nothing worked? You tried reading, resting, eating something, going on a shopping spree, anything you could to try to relieve that agitation. Nothing worked. You still felt that terrible unrest.

God's Spirit can calm that agitation in your soul. I'll be so bold as to say that nothing else will help you. Sure, the activities and substances you try may temporarily relieve pain and pressure, but nothing will give you that deep satisfaction like some Jesus in your soul.

And all you must do is "come to Him." How do you do that? With a sigh, a look in His direction, a prayer, a cry – He hears and sees it all, and He knows when your heart is reaching out to Him. I promise you He will reach right back, instantly!

He is close to the brokenhearted (Psalm 34:18.) He receives us when we boldly approach His throne of grace (Hebrews 4:16.) He is waiting for you to nod, and He will come running to rescue, comfort and fill every place in your heart that needs healing.

How do I know this is true? I've been in this place repeatedly. He has met me every time. He loves you. He wants to spend time with you. He is waiting. Will you come?

Day 272

My Journey So Far

Isaiah 57:15-59:21 / Philippians 1:1-26 / Psalm 71 / Proverbs 24:9-10

I don't often share about how I got where I am, so I feel now is a good time for that. Yes, there were some verses I read today that caused me to consider this, and I'll share those in a bit. When I was born, my mother had received Christ, but my father had not. My father received Jesus when I was about four years old.

My dad spent all his life in the Methodist Church and sadly did not once hear the message about Jesus Christ. I'm not sure what his church taught, and I'm sure not all Methodist churches omit this most basic of messages. My mom didn't have a church growing up. Her home life was tumultuous, and no one in her family knew Jesus Christ.

Somewhere in her teen years, she visited a church with a friend and accepted Jesus as her Savior. The chaos in her life continued, and then she met my dad in that Methodist church, on an Easter Sunday in Sunday school class. This is where my story begins. Sure, there is a bloodline story of faith in Christ that goes much deeper than my parents. I am thankful for the generational blessing of faith in God.

When I was born in 1962, my parents were still attending the Methodist Church. In some home meetings they began attending, my dad received salvation, and they both ended up baptized and filled with Holy Spirit, a new experience for them both. This caused a stir in the Methodist Church, and they began looking for somewhere else to fellowship.

That shift happened when I was around five years old. It was within that same year that I received Jesus Christ as my Savior. I was water baptized at age 7 in the James River in Hampton, Virginia, and I received my first infilling of the Holy Spirit with the evidence of speaking in tongues at the age of 11.

When did I know that I was called to a life of ministry? That is not an easy answer, because that journey has been one that continues to unfold. After many years of pioneering and leading various things, from small groups to worship, the Lord encouraged me to start writing. That is why you're reading this story today. What is my calling? It's time for those verses I mentioned!

"I couldn't begin to count the times you've been there for me. With the skill of a poet, I'll never run out of things to say about how you faithfully kept me from danger. I will come forth in your mighty strength, O my Lord God. I'll tell everyone that you alone are the perfect one. From my childhood you've been my teacher, and I'm still telling everyone of your miracle-wonders! God, now that I'm old and gray, don't walk away. Give me grace to demonstrate to the next generation all your mighty miracles and your excitement, to show them your magnificent power!"— Psalm 71:15-18 in The Passion Translation

Although I'm not yet "old and gray", God has called me to share my life with you, including how God has been involved from the beginning. I also want to share with you how this miracle-working God will impact and change your life. I believe my mandate is to train and equip those around me to do the greater works Jesus talked about. After the training and equipping, expect to be sent out by Holy Spirit into your own adventure and calling!

The work we are part of is one of exponential increase; each generation will increase in strength, power, and love until the coming of Jesus Christ. That final generation will need to be strong indeed because the same clashing of powers we see today will be magnified then. Good and evil will continue to be at war, but the end of the story has already been written. We win.

Thank you for continuing to read as I write and share my heart. My prayer is that my journey allows you to become stronger each day. Stay on the path. Stay connected to Jesus Christ. You will also win!

Day 273

Do You Know Your Life Mandate?

Isaiah 60:1-62:5 / Philippians 1:27-2:18 / Psalm 72 / Proverbs 24:11-12

Do you know the gift and call of God on your life? Do you know the mandate He has given you? Yesterday, I shared parts of my journey. Today I want to share about the calling on my life. I don't remember when I knew, but I knew. Every time I read these verses the Lord highlights them to me. Then a brand-new friend, upon first meeting me, prophesied these same verses over me. I love it when God confirms His word!

"The Spirit of the Sovereign LORD is upon me, for the LORD has anointed me to bring good news to the poor. He has sent me to comfort the brokenhearted and to proclaim that captives will be released, and prisoners will be freed. He has sent me to tell those who mourn that the time of the LORD's favor has come, and with it, the day of God's anger against their enemies. To all who mourn in Israel, he will give a crown of beauty for ashes, a joyous blessing instead of mourning, festive praise instead of despair. In their righteousness, they will be like great oaks that the LORD has planted for his own glory."—Isaiah 61:1-3

I know I'm not the only one with this call. Perhaps this is also your calling; those with similar callings have a way of finding one another. There is a five-part calling and mandate for those who have heard the Isaiah 61 message. I want to list the five mandates, then explain further so you know what God has given you for yourself and others. Remember, the anointing is first for yourself, and then for others.

First, we are told to bring "good news to the poor." What is the good news, and who are the poor? When we bring this good news, we are "preaching salvation" to those who are "weak, afflicted, and needy." Those who are without Christ have nothing of value within them from which to draw. They are left completely alone and without resources. Our first place of service is to bring them the message of Jesus Christ.

Second, we are told to "comfort the brokenhearted." What does comfort look like, and who are the brokenhearted? When we comfort in this way we are bringing "healing to the wounds" of those who have been "shattered or crushed within their soul." I've been in this place and the Lord graciously brought friends into my life who He used to bring healing to my soul. Now I'm bringing healing to the souls of others.

Third, we are told to "proclaim release to captives." What does it mean to be released, and who are the captives? When we proclaim release to captives, we are "speaking aloud the message of freedom to those who have been kidnapped." We must use our words to proclaim out loud freedom for those who have been taken against their will, either physically or emotionally, or both. The real pandemic in our time is trafficking, and we must declare freedom in the Spirit, and find out what we can do in the natural to support the effort toward freedom for those who have been wrongly used. We can no longer say we did not know.

Fourth, we are told to "proclaim that prisoners will be freed." How is that different from freedom for the captives? Let's find out! This is my summation after reading the definitions for "prisoners" and "freed". We are to bring truth that will open the eyes of the one who was taken prisoner by the lies of the enemy. The nature of deception is that the one who is deceived does not realize she is deceived. We must, with the help of Holy Spirit, bring light to this one in darkness.

Fifth, we are told to "tell those who mourn that the Lord's favor has come, and His anger is poured out on their enemies". What is mourning? What is the Lord's favor? And what does it look like for God's anger to be released against our enemies? These are the definitions I concluded after reading from the Strong's Concordance. "Those who are mourning due to the death of someone they love or because of some sort of calamity that entered their lives are to be encouraged that the Lord's favor is being declared over them." God's favor is His "pleasure and delight." It's as if His blessing is being spoken over them even while they are grieving, perhaps meant to draw them through the difficult season.

Finally, what about God's anger being released on our enemies? I'm certainly ready to see some of that, and I'm sure you are as well! The dictionary definition of "vengeance" is "punishment inflicted, or retribution exacted for an injury or wrong."

Remember the scripture that tells us not to seek revenge, and that vengeance belongs to the Lord? (Romans 12:19.) Take that to heart when you've been wronged.

This information is a lot to digest, so I hope you'll read through it again. It helped clarify my calling, so I hope it did the same for you. Be strong in the Lord, and partner with Him to do the things He's given you – those good works He intended for you from before He created you (Ephesians 2:10.)

Biography

Maria Kear began her Jesus journey when she received Christ at the age of five. That dramatic encounter with Him set her up for a life filled with a spiritual hunger that compels her to not only seek after God wholeheartedly, but also to create hunger and thirst in others through her words, experience and life example.

Maria and her husband Jeff have three adult children and as of this writing they have four grandchildren with more promised in the future.

Maria and Jeff launched a house church called Bethesda Springs House of Mercy and Grace in July 2020 when the Lord surprised them with His plans as they fasted and prayed just prior.

Maria has many fond sayings, one of which is, "I want to leave this earth with my hair still on fire!"

May your "hair" catch fire as you read and become hungrier for Him.